ANGELS,
MIRACLES,
AND
HEAVENLY
ENCOUNTERS

Books by
James Stuart Bell

FROM BETHANY HOUSE PUBLISHERS

Angels, Miracles, and Heavenly Encounters
From the Library of A.W. Tozer
From the Library of Charles Spurgeon
Love Is a Flame
The Spiritual World of the Hobbit

ANGELS, MIRACLES,
AND
HEAVENLY ENCOUNTERS

Real-life Stories *of* Supernatural Events

COMPILED BY
JAMES STUART BELL

BETHANY HOUSE PUBLISHERS
a division of Baker Publishing Group
Minneapolis, Minnesota

Published by Bethany House Publishers
11400 Hampshire Avenue South
Bloomington, Minnesota 55438
www.bethanyhouse.com

Bethany House Publishers is a division of
Baker Publishing Group, Grand Rapids, Michigan

Printed in the United States of America

Library of Congress Cataloging-in-Publication Data
    Angels, miracles, and heavenly encounters : real-life stories of supernatural events / compiled by James Stuart Bell.
       p.   cm.
    Summary: "A compilation of true stories of the supernatural—including encounters with angels and demons, near-death experiences, exciting rescues, miraculous provision, and manifestations of God's presence—written from a Christian perspective"—Provided by publisher.
       ISBN 978-0-7642-0958-1 (pbk. : alk. paper)
       1. Christian life—Anecdotes. 2. Supernatural—Anecdotes. 3. Miracles—Anecdotes. I. Bell, James S.
    BV4517.A525 2012
    242—dc23   2012004891

Editorial services provided by Jeanette Gardner Littleton

Cover design by Brand Navigation

12   13   14   15   16   17   18   7   6   5   4

*To my friend of over forty years, Joe Murphy,
who has shared many spiritual adventures with
me, especially the "werewolf" encounter.*

Contents

7

Acknowledgments

I am thankful for the vision of Kyle Duncan, who was willing to deal with the ephemeral territory of extraordinary spiritual experiences. Also, to Julie Smith and Ellen Chalifoux, who provided expert editing and critical judgment on a challenging topic. Thanks also to Jeanette Littleton for her invaluable assistance, and to Andy McGuire and Tim Peterson for their aesthetic input. And to the contributors who were willing to share their most intimate encounters with the supernatural, who prove that God is still working in mysterious and exciting ways.

Introduction

The supernatural world, the world revealed to us in the Scriptures, is normally apprehended by faith and not by our senses. But at times, though they may be few and far between, for God's own mysterious reasons, we are allowed a window into that world. He may be trying to warn us about some danger, encourage our faith, or provide guidance in terms of our behavior.

It is a world of strange marvels, with its own set of rules that go beyond the laws of nature. And even when we get a glimpse of that other world, as the apostle Paul says, we see through a glass darkly. It may be difficult to explain to others what we see or feel in these encounters, and perplexing when we try to interpret their full meaning. Some of these experiences may be meant as special gifts to be cherished alone, others to be shared to edify others.

This volume of supernatural stories attempts to achieve the latter purpose. In sharing these very personal experiences,

13

the writers herein hope to convey how much God cares for us and how active and close He is to us—fighting our battles and revealing the eternal consequences of our choices and behavior, even our thoughts and attitudes, here on earth.

It is true that we normally live by faith and not by sight, but some of us at certain times are given supernatural sight, hearing, and even smell. The supernatural world constantly intersects our fallen world but manifests itself at key times: during intense spiritual warfare, at the time of death, when we're in mortal danger or dire need, and when God wants to reveal His glory. So it isn't surprising that these stories involve angels and demons, near-death experiences, exciting rescues, miraculous provision, and manifestations of God's presence in worship.

We know that one day all the stress and struggle will be over, as we personally go to be with the Lord after death, and finally when He returns in glory. This shadowland will be a fading memory, and He will wipe all tears from our eyes. But even now we live in the victory of His cross and resurrection, and we know that He has equipped us for the work of His kingdom. And whether or not we personally experience the supernatural as in these stories, we can benefit from those who have sampled a taste of it.

When God seems far from us and the natural world feels like the only world, we can be encouraged that the God who pulled back the curtain for a moment in the lives of these writers to reveal His power is the same God who works more silently at all times for our good.

James Stuart Bell

ANGELS,
MIRACLES,
AND
HEAVENLY
ENCOUNTERS

The Good-Bye Promise

TAMARA L. STAGG

"That's good, Pawpaw. You're eating mashed potatoes!" Derek said as he moved his grandfather's chin up and down, up and down.

Pawpaw might have smiled, if he'd had more control of his muscles. Instead, he let his jaw fall open for another bite, his jaundiced gaze fixed intently on my eleven-year-old son.

They were twins, Derek and Pawpaw, different only in age and experience. As Derek raised another spoonful of potatoes to Pawpaw's lips, their profiles mirrored each other's perky ears, rounded cheeks, slender necks, and curved shoulders.

I looked out the window at the Mayo Clinic grounds. A mature display of green oak leaves mimicked my stillness. Even creation seemed to know that Derek and Pawpaw would soon be separated. They would no longer fidget with electronic gadgets together, join hands on the steering wheel of Pawpaw's boat, or walk side-by-side with the same gait to check the mail or walk the dogs or visit the neighbors.

"Derek," I said, several weeks after Pawpaw stopped eating, "do you understand that medicine cannot help Pawpaw anymore?"

A shrug of acceptance. "Yeah, I understand that."

Blinking tears away, I steered my son's slender shoulders closer to Pawpaw's bedside. "You should say good-bye to him now, honey. He might not live through the night."

Derek stared at the dangling tubes that had recently been disconnected. Then he eyed the severely bruised and punctured skin of his grandfather. Heavy doses of steroids, antibiotics, and other treatments had only prolonged Pawpaw's battle against vasculitis of the brain.

Pawpaw watched Derek with yellow-glazed, half-opened eyes.

After several moments, Derek said, "I can't say good-bye now, Mama. It doesn't make sense. He's not leaving yet."

I wrapped my arms around Derek's shoulders. "Yes, he's still here, and I think he hears every word," I said. "But he could go any minute, and how will you feel if he dies before you say good-bye?"

Derek shook his head adamantly. "I'll say good-bye when he leaves."

I cringed. Throughout Pawpaw's illness, I'd struggled with how to guide my children's prayers. "If it's your will" was a phrase I'd turned to often, knowing that God's plans sometimes differ from our greatest hopes.

But Derek did not preface his heartfelt request with "If it's your will." He kept saying boldly to God, "Please let me say good-bye to Pawpaw when he leaves."

"At least tell Pawpaw you love him before we go for the night," I suggested now.

This, he could do.

"I love you, Pawpaw," he said tenderly.

As days passed, Derek and my nine-year-old daughter, Haley, supported Pawpaw by sitting with him and telling him stories. If he heard them, his blank stare showed no sign of it. Each time Derek left Pawpaw's side, he said, "I love you," but never good-bye.

One afternoon I took my children out of the hospital room for a little break. When we rejoined relatives in Pawpaw's room, his breathing had slowed dramatically. I looked at the clock and saw that he was inhaling only about once every twenty to thirty seconds.

"He's going," I warned my husband.

We all huddled around Pawpaw's bed. Each time we thought we'd seen his last breath he surprised us with one more inhalation. After several minutes of this, his lungs stopped for more than fifty seconds. Sixty seconds. Seventy seconds. Eighty.

Pawpaw's favorite nurse, a Christian, entered the room and watched with us.

I felt tears sting my eyes and choke my throat. This was it. Pawpaw was gone.

We all began to grieve more openly—all except Derek, who said cheerfully, "Bye, Pawpaw!"

I glanced over at him and saw that he was staring at the ceiling with a smile spread wide across his face.

He just got his wish, I realized.

But why was he looking up to say good-bye instead of saying it to Pawpaw's still face?

The head resident entered the room and confirmed the death.

I moved toward Derek, drawn to his pure joy and puzzled by it.

"I saw Pawpaw go!" he exclaimed.

The nurse rushed toward us. "I'd like to hear this, if you don't mind," she said. "Children really do see things sometimes."

"Did you see something?" I asked Derek.

"Uh-huh. Pawpaw was on the ceiling."

My brows shot up. "On the ceiling? You mean he was floating?"

"Nooo." Derek laughed at me. "There were hands lifting him up!"

"Hands?" I glanced at the nurse.

She clamped her hands together. "What else did you see?" she asked.

Derek's broad smile never wavered. "He was dressed in a bright white robe, and he looked a lot younger. He had a lot more hair, and his skin looked really smooth, without any spots. And his face looked happier than ever. He looked at me and waved and said, 'Bye, Derek!' and I waved back and said, 'Bye, Pawpaw!'"

Derek's face beamed up at me. "He looked so happy, Mama. You've never seen him look so happy!"

"Were they Jesus' hands?" I asked, trying to make sense of this.

A shrug. "I couldn't tell. I could only see the fingers. But they were bright white like the robe—really bright."

"What made you think to look up at the ceiling?" I asked.

"Pawpaw was talking to his daddy a few days ago," Derek said, "like he could see him in heaven. I've been looking up because I wanted to see him too. I never could see him, but I got to see Pawpaw waving at me."

The nurse must have sensed my skepticism, because she said, "This is real. This happens with some children. They get to see Jesus take their loved ones away." Placing a hand on Derek's shoulder, she added, "I'm so happy for your Pawpaw, I've got goose bumps!"

"God answered your prayer," I said to Derek.

He chuckled. "Yeah, God let me say good-bye at the right time, but I didn't expect Pawpaw to wave and say good-bye to me too!"

"That was quite a bonus," I said, still watching my son. He kept speaking of Pawpaw's happiness, but I'd never seen Derek look so happy.

Thank you, God, for giving them one last pleasure together, I prayed. *And please forgive me for doubting the power of your love. You're probably as tickled by all of this as they are—maybe more so.*

Derek's good cheer lasted until the funeral services. He did not like seeing Pawpaw in a casket. But an easy remedy for his sadness seemed to come at just the right times. Each time a frown formed on his lips, one of Pawpaw's Sunday school students or neighbors or relatives wanted to hear Derek's testimony.

"I heard you saw your Pawpaw leave," Derek heard over and over. Each time his face lit up, and his gleeful response reaffirmed that Jesus will one day carry us to heaven, that God's promises are credible, and that we've not seen the last of Christians who have gone before us.

Surprise Attack

David Milotta

As a pastor I've found that death is never easy to deal with. It's especially difficult for Christians when a family member who doesn't know Christ says his or her final good-byes.

But as I walked into the little room, I had no idea just how difficult this funeral was going to be. I had been ministering to one of our church families through their loved one's death. The deceased was Buddhist and the service was to be conducted by the *bonsan* (priest) at the *hongwaji* (church) near Kona, Hawaii.

The Buddhist church was modeled after the ancient temples of Kyoto, Japan, with sturdy, ornately carved wooden beams and a steep red tile roof with upturned corners.

As I bowed my head to enter, I adroitly avoided the low eaves that seemed aimed for my forehead. Mine was the only white face present.

This building was not designed for tall people, I thought as I squeezed my lanky frame into an ancient wooden pew in the back row of the sanctuary.

My eyes slowly adjusted to the dim light as my ears and nose processed the strange sounds and aromas of the temple.

In the front I saw a simple wooden altar with a brass urn upon it that held the ashes of the deceased. The cloying smell of burning incense mixed with the spicy sweetness of the pikake lei that was draped around the framed picture of the deceased.

The congregation was chanting something that sounded like "Ohn ran ji go." This rumbling sound was punctuated with the hollow gonging of a five-foot-tall, elongated bell as it was struck with a swinging, thick bamboo pole.

I had attended Buddhist funeral services before, but this time I suppressed feelings of great alarm. Some unknown force drew my attention to the golden statue of Buddha behind the right side of the altar.

Usually, Buddha is portrayed as a jolly, smiling, fat man with pendulous earlobes. This one was solemn with eight arms like the Hindu god Shiva, the destroyer.

I heard the *bonsan* call to each family head and visitor to come forward to the front altar and offer incense.

Beware, there's danger here, an inner voice warned as I wiggled out of the pew and walked to the altar to pay my respects.

I felt eyes upon me, questioning, *What is this* gaijin *(foreigner) doing here?*

I chose not to light incense, as it is an offering to a false god. Instead, I planned to offer a silent prayer in front of the altar.

As I approached the altar I felt that God was saying to me, "I want you to pray for the soul of the deceased, and pray that this building and everybody in it be covered with the blood of Jesus."

The blood of Jesus I understand, but the dead are already gone, so why bother?

I put my questions aside and silently prayed in front of the altar.

Suddenly, I saw a terrifying form jump out from inside the statue of Buddha and head straight for my throat!

I was frozen in shock.

The demon—for it could be nothing else—was a greenish luminescent orb about the size of a basketball with a comet-like tail. It had a fierce dragon face with bared fangs and claws. It radiated hatred, rage, and intimidation. It seemed like it wanted to kill me.

"God help me," I desperately prayed.

Just then I felt as though God sent His angels to surround me, as if they encased me in angelic Plexiglas.

The demon seemed to hit the angelic shield, bounce off, and disappear in an instant. I returned to my seat in bewilderment and disbelief.

I thought, *That didn't really happen. You're working too hard. You're imagining things.*

After the service we moved to the social hall for a traditional Buddhist meal. During the meal, a complete stranger introduced himself. He was a middle-aged, average-looking Japanese man in a business suit.

As he handed me his business card, he said, "I am a brother-in-law of the deceased and a recent convert to Christianity. I am the only believer in my family and attend a Pentecostal Holiness church in Honolulu. We have a deliverance ministry. I want you to know that I saw that demon attack you, and I was praying for you the whole time.

"I have the gift of spiritual discernment and I often see demons on people," he continued.

I could hardly believe what I was hearing. My mind was not playing tricks on me. Here was independent verification from an outside source. What I thought was some gross hallucination on my part was really a demonic attack. The demon was probably attracted to the statue of Buddha, as it was the focus of adoration, prayer, and chanting. When I prayed "The blood of Jesus cover this building and everybody in it," apparently the spiritual effect was like spraying supernatural bug spray on an unholy cockroach. The demon fled and attacked me out of its rage over losing its protective host.

I've heard many stories of missionaries encountering such experiences in foreign lands. That day I learned it also happens in my own beloved country. But I also learned that even when I am unexpectedly ambushed by a demon, God sends His angels to protect me.

A Secret for Five

PAM ZOLLMAN

I knew a secret. Only three people—maybe four—knew this secret: me; my husband, Bill; his secretary, Jill; and maybe Jill's husband.

And what was that secret?

Bill, my husband of nearly thirty years, wanted to divorce me and marry Jill.

Divorce is nothing new; it was going on even in Jesus' time. It wasn't even new to me. My mother has been married numerous times, divorcing my own father when I was two.

But I had never envisioned myself divorced. Bill and I still held hands! Well, we did until February 14, 2001. That stopped after a romantic dinner at our favorite restaurant when he announced that he was moving out.

"Nothing you say or do will change my mind," Bill said.

Valentine's Day had always been important to Bill. While he might not always remember my birthday or our anniversary, he always remembered February 14 and made it special. He proposed to me on Valentine's Day, giving me flowers, treating me to dinner, and getting down on one knee after a stroll on the beach.

On the twenty-fifth anniversary of his proposal, he gave me a gold heart with a diamond at the center.

"Wear this always and it will remind you of my love," he said.

On Valentine's night in 2001, I sat in shock, fingering the heart necklace I always wore and wondering how long our marriage had been a joke. I had not seen this coming.

I chose not to tell anyone about my husband's affair, especially not our two sons, because I was praying that Bill would change his mind. And if he did, I didn't want any of my friends or family members to hold his indiscretion against him. I loved him and was willing to forgive him. Plus, I think I was in denial. If I kept quiet about it, then it might not actually happen.

So a few days later when I went to the post office, the secret was still a secret.

When I got to the post office parking lot, I had about five minutes before the employees closed the doors. Another woman had pulled into the space next to mine. She struggled with three large boxes, obviously ready to mail.

"Let me help you," I said, taking a box.

"Thank you," she replied with a pronounced Hispanic accent. Her long black hair was pulled back at the sides and fastened with gold clips, and she wore an expensive dark green jacket and matching slacks, as if she'd just gotten off work. Large gold earrings matched her hair clips, and her makeup was perfect.

I, on the other hand, wore jeans and a sweater. My own dark hair was in a long braid down my back. In Houston, Texas, we have mild winters, so neither of us needed a coat.

She gripped a box in either arm and followed me into the post office, her heels clicking on the pavement. My tennis shoes scuffled. A postal employee locked the doors behind us.

As we joined the end of the short line, she asked me about postage.

"I am not from here," she said. A light citrus fragrance surrounded her. "I do not know how to mail these boxes."

"If you're not in a hurry for the packages to arrive, then it's pretty cheap to mail them. But if you want them to arrive by a certain date, then you'll have to pay more for first class or priority mail," I said, shifting her box so I was balancing it on my hip. To the best of my knowledge, I explained the difference between the rates. "And the postal workers here are easy to work with. They'll help you."

As we moved up in line, she told me she was from Guatemala. "Our postal system is not very reliable."

"We complain about ours," I said, "but, overall, it works pretty well."

Two spots opened up at the counter and I handed her the box I was carrying for her.

"Thank you," she said. "I appreciate your help."

I smiled. "No problem."

The woman behind the counter took my large brown envelope, weighed it, and stamped it. I paid for the postage and headed for the door. When the Guatemalan woman stepped away from the counter right behind me, I was surprised. I figured that it would take her longer because of the three boxes, but I was wrong. The postal worker was in a hurry to go home, I guessed.

Another employee unlocked the door and let us out.

"You've been so helpful," she said as we walked out together. "I would like to do something for you now."

"Oh, goodness, no," I protested. "I didn't really do anything."

"Would you let me pray for you?" she asked.

"Pray for me?" That surprised me. As a Christian I had no problem with people praying for me, but a stranger had never offered to pray for me in a parking lot. I hesitated for only a moment.

"Sure," I said.

She stood in front of me and took both of my hands in hers. A charm bracelet jingled on her right wrist. Rings adorned several fingers and her nails were painted pale pink. I closed my eyes as she began to pray.

"Heavenly Father, I lift up Pam—"

Pam. I didn't remember telling her my name . . . but, maybe I had?

"—and ask that you give her strength and courage to face her current situation."

My current situation? What?

"Give her and her two sons the guidance they'll need."

My two sons? I knew I'd never mentioned my family to her.

"And surround her with your love during the divorce and afterward."

My eyes flew open and I stared at her. Her eyes were still closed and her face serene. How could she know any of this about me?

"Help her to know that the future holds great hope for her. Through Jesus Christ I pray. Amen."

She opened her eyes and smiled at me, squeezing my hands.

I was so astonished, I didn't know what to say.

She unhooked her charm bracelet and fastened it around my right wrist. "I want you to have this."

"Oh, no," I said, "I couldn't possibly—"

She raised a hand, and I stopped speaking. "I want you to wear this. It will remind you of God's love for you."

I looked at the charm bracelet as my left hand fingered my necklace. Almost the exact words Bill had said to me five years earlier.

Eyeing my hand on the heart necklace, she shook her head.

"This isn't a promise like that one," she said. "This is God's promise to you. He loves you and wants you to be reminded of it, especially during the tough times that are ahead of you."

"How . . . how do you know these things?" I asked.

"Don't worry about that," she said with a smile. "Accept the gift and know that God loves you."

"Thank you," I said. I held my arm up and the charm bracelet jingled like tiny bells. "Could I have your name and phone number? I . . . I might want to talk to you again."

"Sure," she said and dug in her black purse. She scribbled her name and phone number on a torn piece of pink paper and handed it to me.

I wanted to be sure I wouldn't lose it, so I put it in the coin section of my wallet.

"Thank you," I repeated.

She waved good-bye, got in her car, and drove off. I stood in the parking lot, staring at the bracelet.

The bracelet was silver in color but was not an expensive piece of jewelry. The charms were set in three sets of threes. Each set had a leaping dolphin facing right, a star, and a leaping dolphin facing left. Nothing Christian about it. And yet, I felt special wearing it.

I drove home wondering about my strange encounter. Once

at home, I opened the coin section of my wallet to look at that pink piece of paper. But it wasn't there. I have no idea what happened to it, but it disappeared between the post office and my home.

Was the Guatemalan woman an angel in disguise? I have no idea, but I like to think she was. Even if she wasn't an angel, God was obviously using her. She was no ordinary woman. She knew my secret.

And so did God.

That comforted me during the divorce and the years after. All I had to do was look at that bracelet to know that God loved me; He cared what happened to me, and He was with me. Always.

A Supernatural Shove

EMILY SECOMB, as told to
CHERYL SECOMB

My senior year in high school I auditioned for a role in the school's fall production. That year we were performing Neil Simon's comedy *Fools*. At tryouts, the drama teacher who would cast and direct the play had us read from different roles in the script.

I connected with one of the lead roles, Sophia, and hoped I would be chosen for the part. I eagerly waited for the day the cast list would be posted.

On that day I held my breath as I approached the bulletin board. I scanned the list until I found my name. Next to it was typed the character's name: *Sophia*.

I got the part!

"Thank you, Lord!" I whispered.

None of us who were in the play had ever heard of it before our auditions, but we soon found it to be a hilarious script and fun to perform. The play is set around 1890 in a village called Kulyenchikov. The people there are placed under a curse of stupidity. My character, Sophia, is especially stupid.

When a new teacher, Leon, comes to town, he falls in love with Sophia and believes he can break the curse by teaching her. He learns that unless he can teach her something within twenty-four hours, he also will fall under the curse and become as stupid as the rest of the townspeople.

The play became so popular with the school audience that many parents and students returned to watch it for more than one performance.

I was having the time of my life—except for one thing. In one scene, Leon stood beneath the balcony I stood on. As Sophia, I invited him to climb the trellis to reach me, but as he did so I ran down to where he was standing.

From above, a frustrated Leon would tell me to wait for him to come down. But knowing I would run upstairs once again, he waited on the balcony as I raced back up.

Each time, the audience erupted in laughter. The scene was one of our favorites, but it was difficult to maneuver. During the scene, I rushed down from the balcony backstage and around to enter onstage, said my lines, and then raced to the balcony again backstage. During this sprint, I had to jump over a small gap between the balcony set and the stage. I was nervous about tripping, especially since I had to move quickly to reach the balcony on cue.

The set was sturdy, but because I could see to the floor below, my fear of heights was magnified. No one else had trouble with the spot and I was too embarrassed to mention that I did.

I made it through rehearsals and opening night without a glitch, but the second night brought near disaster. As part of my costume, I wore short boots with heels. They weren't the easiest to walk in, let alone run.

That night I'd said my lines from the balcony, sprinted to the stage, delivered my lines there, and raced back to the balcony for the next scene. This time as I leaped across the gap, my foot hit the edge of the narrow platform.

Suddenly, my balance was gone. I jolted backwards!

I vaguely realized that metal objects were behind me—stabilizers or supporters of some kind. Whatever they were, I was falling and my head was aimed directly toward them!

I'm going to die!

My arms flailed like windmills as I struggled to regain my balance. No luck. I was tipped back to the point of no return.

Suddenly, some force shoved against the center of my back, propelling me forward three to four feet. I landed quietly and directly in front of the curtain where I was to enter the balcony on cue.

My heart pounded, adrenaline pumping through my body.

I turned to see who had helped me by pushing me forward, but no one was there.

Somehow, though my whole body shook, I managed to finish the balcony scene. I ran backstage and saw my friend in the hall.

"Michael, did you see that?"

"What?"

"I almost fell and something pushed me!" I explained what had happened.

"Really?" He studied my face for a moment, then smiled. "That's awesome!"

After the performance, I told the other cast members about my experience. They affirmed that none of them had come to my rescue. In fact, they were amazed and didn't quite know what to think of my story.

The rest of the performances flowed smoothly. After that night, a teacher stood at the gap and helped me, making sure I wouldn't trip again. The production was a success.

I've thought much about this experience since that night. I realize that it couldn't have been a person who rescued me because that person would have caught me—not shoved me forward—and I would have seen him or her.

I believe that God protected me that night. Did God himself deliver me with the force I felt, or was it an unseen angel He placed there to protect me? I don't know, but I'm reminded of how in 2 Kings 6, God opened Elisha's servant's eyes to see the mountain full of horses and chariots of fire around them. If God were to open our eyes, would we see a heavenly host surrounding us today?

I'm still amazed and humbled that such an experience would happen to someone like me. I find comfort in the thought that as He delivered me that night, He will always protect me.

The Silent Cry
That Was Heard

SALLY BURBANK

Applause thundered across the dimly lit dinner theater as we *Godspell* thespians bowed triumphantly to the standing ovation. When the clapping subsided, we bounded off the stage and bee-lined to the dressing room.

"That was the best audience ever," I exclaimed to Claire, another actress in the show.

"You sure wowed them with your solo, 'All Good Gifts.' It sent shivers down my spine."

"Thanks," I said as I smeared cold cream over my face to scrub off the heavy stage makeup.

When my face was clean, I searched for the girl who always offered me a ride home. "Has anybody seen Deb?"

"Deb? She left with Robert to grab a bite after the show," a cast member replied.

My shoulders sagged. How would I get home now? I lived four miles from the theater, and no buses ran at this time of night. Straight out of college, I couldn't afford a taxi. Worse still, the theater was located in a bad part of town littered with smoky bars and street people. None of the other cast members lived near me, so I hesitated to beg for a ride.

I changed into jeans and a T-shirt and mulled over my dilemma. Maybe an invigorating walk home would unwind me from the excitement of the show and from my jitters about tomorrow's high school reunion. I was anxious to face everyone after five years.

I'd been a pudgy honor student in high school. I lived for a cappella madrigals, debate team, and Jane Austen novels. Stir in my church choir commitment and pitiful finish in every cross-country running meet, and no one could have found a better poster child for "Miss Montpelier Nerd."

Now I eyed this reunion as my chance to reveal all I had accomplished since graduation. I envisioned confronting Robby Sorenson, the bully who had tortured me with his taunts of "Tub-of-lard" and "Fatso." I salivated at the image of parading my curly-haired fiancé and slimmed-down physique in front of him. I'd casually drop comments about performing to standing ovation crowds, graduating from college summa cum laude, and entering medical school in the fall.

"So what have you been up to, Robby?" I'd dig, knowing his crowning achievement since high school was a two-bit job pumping gas. Rumor had it that his girlfriend had recently dumped him, so I'd be sure to ask about her. It would serve him right.

I plodded toward home, gloating in my daydreams, oblivious to the stranger who lurked behind me. Gradually, however, I could feel his breath heavy on my neck.

What's his deal?

My heart began to pound. Cars whipped by and fraternity houses bustled with noise.

Surely he won't attack me on the busiest street in Burlington.

Still, the guy made me nervous, so I stepped aside and gestured for him to pass by.

"I'm obviously slowing you down, so why don't you go ahead of me?" I said in a shaky voice.

He grunted and plowed ahead. I dawdled until he was a healthy distance ahead of me, and then I crossed the street to get even farther away from him. I sighed in relief and scolded myself for my paranoia. He was probably just some college student so distracted by his own worries that he was clueless about the panic he'd ignited in me.

I veered onto the secluded street where I lived. After a four-mile trek, my feet ached and I was more than ready to flop into bed. Just six houses to go and I'd be home.

Suddenly, my mouth was clamped in a vice-like grip. Arms like those of a giant octopus snatched me from behind and dragged me off the sidewalk. I immediately recognized my assailant as the creep who'd stalked me earlier. He must have doubled back and followed me down the dead-end street.

I kicked and fought and bit and clawed in a futile attempt to escape, but I was no match for this madman. He shoved me to the ground behind a stone fence.

I suddenly remembered that just one month earlier, a girl my age had been raped, strangled, and murdered behind a stone fence on a quiet street just like this one. The local newspaper had printed a picture of the man with whom she had last been seen, and he looked frighteningly similar to this man.

I'm about to be raped and murdered, just like that girl!

I jerked my head away and let out a blood-curdling scream. I opened my mouth to release another roof-raiser, but he slammed my jaw shut.

"Shut up! Shut up or I'll kill you."

He ripped off my T-shirt and jammed it into my mouth as a gag. He stretched out my arms and pinned them down, and he tugged at my jeans while his knees pinned my legs to the ground.

My heart pounded at a dizzying rate.

This can't be happening! I don't want to die. Somebody rescue me!

But no one came. In a last-ditch effort to escape, I jerked upward, but he smashed me to the ground and tightened his grip on my arms. He glared into my eyes and spewed, "You're not going anywhere. I've just started in on you."

My heart pounded like a kettledrum.

What was I going to do? I couldn't overpower this psychopath. And with a gag in my mouth, I couldn't scream.

But you can pray, a voice whispered in my head.

Help me! I'm about to be raped! I pleaded silently to my only source of hope. Over and over I petitioned God with this same prayer, knowing I was powerless, but He was not.

My attacker loosened his trousers. I suddenly heard footsteps pounding down the sidewalk.

"Leave her alone! Leave her alone," a man's voice shouted.

As the sound of running feet neared, my assailant bolted through the bushes.

A man clad in pajama bottoms and loafers peeked over the fence.

"Are you all right?" he panted and helped me to my feet.

I burst into tears. "Thank you so much for coming. You saved my life."

I clutched his arm, never so grateful to meet a complete stranger in my life.

He escorted me to his house, where his wife gave me an untorn T-shirt and a mug of chamomile tea to calm my frazzled nerves.

While we waited for the police to arrive, we rehashed the events of my attack. But then my hero dropped a bombshell. "When I heard you holler, 'Help me! I'm about to be raped!' I knew I had to come."

My heart lurched. "But you couldn't have heard me say that. I was gagged."

He scratched his head. "Well, I don't understand it, but I clearly heard a voice say, 'Help me! I'm about to be raped!'"

His wife piped in. "The weird thing is, I never heard it, and I was lying in bed right next to him. But he insisted he'd heard it, so he bolted for the door."

My heart stopped. "Those were the exact words I prayed in my mind."

We stared at one another in stunned shock. How was it possible? Had he read my mind?

It didn't make sense, but apparently God had transferred my desperate prayer into this man's brain, just as though he had heard the words audibly.

I spent the next several hours providing a police report. I never made it to that high school reunion; I was too preoccupied with the Burlington Crime Stoppers unit to attend the festivities. But somehow, I no longer cared. My life had nearly been snuffed out, but God had miraculously allowed me to live.

The next time I belted out my solo, "All good gifts around us are sent from heaven above," I marveled at how true those lyrics had been for me.

Truly He does send us good gifts!

Seeing Things
in a Different Light

TINA SAMPLES

Kenneth had just been drafted into World War II. Faye, my mother, stood at the door and waved good-bye to her eighteen-year-old brother.

After his training he was sent to Germany. Three months later my mother and grandparents received word that my Uncle Kenneth had been shot. A German sniper shot him through his left temple, severing his optic nerve. The bullet exited through his right eye—taking the eye with it.

The military paid for my grandmother to go and stay with my uncle during his long, strenuous recovery. He spent a difficult, painful year at a hospital in Virginia recovering from his wounds. He then spent another year learning how to live with no sight. How does such a young man face the rest of his life with no sight?

Two years passed before my fourteen-year-old mother got to see her brother.

"Kenneth!" she exclaimed when she saw him.

"Come here, Faye, and let me see you," he said.

"But you can't see," my mom pointed out.

"Oh, I can—just in a different way," he explained.

My mother stood in front of him and my uncle placed his hands on her shoulders.

"My you've grown."

She smiled. He took one hand and found her head—touching the soft curls of her chestnut brown hair.

"You're getting tall!"

He then slid his hands down the sides of her face, cupping her cheeks in his palms. With the tips of his fingers he gently touched her lips, nose, and eyes.

"You're beautiful!"

My mother's heart sank, and she couldn't stand it any longer. She grabbed her brother. "I am so glad you are home!"

The next Sunday Uncle Kenneth went to church with the family. Though his life had changed, one thing would remain the same—going to church. The church members were all happy to see Uncle Kenneth and praised God that he had come home alive.

Toward the end of the service, people gathered around my uncle and placed their hands upon him. They came before the Lord and pleaded for his sight. They prayed and prayed—asking God to restore his vision.

Their intercession was strong and earnest. And when it was all over, Uncle Kenneth raised his head, opened his eyes, and received his sight!

Gasping, the people cried out, thanking God for Uncle Kenneth's sight. Cheers and roars could be heard down the street.

Uncle Kenneth turned to my grandmother and exclaimed, "You're beautiful!"

He turned to my grandfather and said, "I didn't know you lost your hair."

My grandfather had lost his hair from a stroke a year before.

Kenneth turned to his friends and called their names one by one. He could see!

That afternoon the family gathered for a big Texas lunch. The table was layered with fried chicken, homemade macaroni and cheese, and freshly baked bread. Smells of apple and pecan pie wafted through the air. Colorful fruit salad, potato salad, and greens rested on the counter. Just the sight of it set stomachs grumbling.

Uncle Kenneth savored every aroma and every element. He had missed the home-cooked meals and the Sunday afternoon gatherings.

Mom's fifteen brothers and sisters were there along with their families. One by one Uncle Kenneth looked at them and soaked in every feature. He walked around the big house and happily rubbed his hands over the cabinets he helped build. He touched everything as he would as if he were blind—but this time soaking it in with his sight.

He wrestled and tickled his niece and nephews. He laughed and joked around. He took his guitar and played with his siblings like in the old days. Melodies of all kinds rang out from the house. The celebration of his sight became a feast that continued into the evening.

After everyone said their good-byes, my uncle took a walk in the cool of the evening around the house—finally coming to the rose garden. Choking back tears, he swallowed hard and touched the delicate petals. Before he'd left for the war, he'd helped his mother plant the rose garden. The flowers were now in full bloom. Red, yellow, white, and deep purple roses adorned the garden. What a glorious sight!

Uncle Kenneth breathed deeply and inhaled the sweet aroma. It filled his body and brightened his soul. Thankfulness and praise poured forth from his lips and radiated toward the heavens. He was in heaven. This was heaven.

As the sun set on that day, so did the light in my Uncle Kenneth's eyes. His sight left him.

For just a brief time the Lord let my uncle see his friends and family. For a few moments, the Lord allowed my uncle to see the sweet rose garden. For just a short time the Lord gave sight to someone who could not see.

No one could explain it. Physically he was not able to see. With no right eye and a severed optic nerve on the other side, sight was just not physically possible. The Lord did not heal him completely. But for a brief time He gave sight to the blind.

It was a gift—a celebration of life and a reminder that God is still gracious even when we experience devastation. Uncle Kenneth was given the blessing of physically seeing his family one last time and visually capturing snapshots of love.

My uncle was blind for the rest of his life. He eventually married a young woman who was also blind. Together they learned to see all things in a different light—even God. Their sight of the most holy God grew brighter than ever.

Was It a Werewolf?

JAMES STUART BELL

We were bouncing along a state highway in Pennsylvania in the late summer of 1973 on the way home to New Jersey, and my mind was shrouded in apprehension. As a college student, I had become a Christian only a few months before, and now I was wondering why much of my initial get-up-and-go peace and joy had got up and went. I wasn't suffering from a serious trial and was still rejoicing in my new salvation, but I felt a vague sense of foreboding, a heaviness that wasn't exactly depression but more like oppression. I had been deeply involved in drugs and the occult and felt like the remnants were still clinging to me.

My friend Joe, who, like me had taken a journey through the occult to Jesus, informed me that although the devil no longer had power over me, he wasn't happy that I had been set free from his dominion and I could cause his domain some future trouble. In other words, I was a demonic target in a way that I had not been in the past when I was the devil's duped servant.

We had begun our trip with my physical healing in mind. Our prayer leader had a gift of healing, and I knew from past involvement in the occult that miracles of a supernatural nature were possible. I had a hip replacement due to a bone tumor and wanted to throw my cane away and run in the fields with the wind at my back.

She suggested a shrine up in Canada where there was a wall of canes and crutches from people healed of their maladies. And although I did not receive a brand-new hip, we still had a soothing time on our way back, staying in Laurentides Park near the St. Lawrence River in Quebec. We slept on open ground and stared at the crowded stars that suddenly put on an aurora borealis display for us—blue and green and moving mighty fast. On the journey we had also decided to burn some record albums like Led Zeppelin and Black Sabbath that, at least for us, had produced some bad fruit. Going to the shrine we probably both looked like a couple of homeless people with our long hair and scraggly jeans.

But all those experiences weren't enough to bring back the peace and joy I coveted. Joe assured me that on our way home we would stop by his campus in Pennsylvania, and his Christian fellowship would pray for my deliverance from oppression. It was now late and we were both tired, so he suggested we get out the sleeping bags and pull over into an enclosed area off the side of the road surrounded by trees.

The moon peeking in between the trees gave us limited light, and as we spread out the sleeping bags, I felt nature call. But I was feeling other mischievous forces calling as well and was nervous about the thirty-yard walk in the dim moonlight to the outhouse in the distance.

As I arrived at the outhouse, I slowly opened the door to make sure no malevolent creatures or people were inside, and sat down on the stool. I noticed a small window on the upper right hand wall and then heard a rustling noise in the bushes outside. It could be anything or anyone, and it could be after me. I didn't want to give myself away and open the door, so I decided to peer through the small window to check what was behind the noises.

What I saw immediately staring back at me was so frightening, I quickly grabbed my pants with one hand and my cane with the other. Joe was by the car preparing our scaled-down campsite when he was startled by a cry of horror and the sound of a door flying open. The moon shone on a frantic figure with long hair wildly flying and a cane moving swiftly up and down toward him.

"I've just seen a werewolf!" I screamed.

Now he was sure I needed a demonic deliverance. But as I drew nearer, I stopped in my tracks, tilted my head, and put my hand on my chin, stroking my beard.

"Wait, that was me!"

From the depths of my being came a howl of laughter. As I was still ten yards away, Joe was beginning to think he needed to get me to his campus prayer group quickly. But I was quite in my right mind.

I had just realized that the outline of the features and growth of hair that I had seen looked a lot like me. Joe had described me, with my dark features and eyes, as a Christian version of Charles Manson, the serial killer. What I thought was a small window in the outhouse that I looked through to check the strange noises was really a small mirror! We both laughed until we fell asleep, and the next day I received copious prayer from his friends at college to lift the oppression caused by my spiritual enemy. I went home feeling free again and decided it was time to get a hair trim, much to the relief of my parents, who had to live with me during that summer.

It's not that long hair or beards are wrong, but what I needed was to discard more of the old Jim and put on the new nature, renewed in the image of Christ. When we least expect it, that old nature that we thought we had vanquished can pop out and scare us.

We will be sinners to the day we die, and that sin will at times hurt ourselves and others. But we have the assurance that God is both forgiving and perfecting us as we cooperate with His grace. I'm a good bit older now and the outward man doesn't have the youthful vigor, but the wasting away is accompanied by the unceasing sanctification of the new me.

Barefoot Rescue

◆——◆

CONNIE GREEN, as told to
CHARLES D. COCHRAN

My husband, Tim, and I feel the outdoors is God's
delightful treasure—that's why we love Colorado.
We travel there several times a year from our native Kansas City to ski, hike, camp, fish, and do anything else
outdoors. It's a heavenly place.

But one trip opened my eyes to a spiritual dimension I
never took seriously before.

For years our two boys had asked to go white-water rafting,
so when they were finally old enough, we booked a one-day
trip. Colorado is famous for the sunny, clear blue skies that
prevailed that morning. We checked in and were soon shuttled
to the launch site on the Arkansas River.

"Your brochure says, 'Scouting may be advisable,'" Tim
said to our guide during the brief safety course before the
trip. "What does that mean?"

"As you know, any white-water trip has its risks. However, this time of year, we go down the river almost daily, so we're usually aware of any hazards," our guide answered. "You needn't worry; it's reasonably safe."

Fair enough—or so we thought.

During the first stage of the trip, the rapids were thrilling and the scenery—when we were able to look at it—showed us snow-laced granite peaks and varying species of lofty pines, a number of them growing directly out of the rocks.

Some of this area is accessible only by river, and the place where we stopped for lunch was so peaceful and relaxing, I could have stayed there the rest of the day. But alas, the rapids were calling. The ride continued with just the right mix of rapids and relatively calm, flowing waters—until . . .

The river narrowed and the rapids increased as we rounded a bend. We were almost on top of the newly fallen tree before we saw it. Immediately our raft was pinned by the force of the water and we were in danger of being swamped or flipped.

"Highside, highside!" shouted our guide.

We paused for a split second as we tried to recall the safety training we received that morning. It seemed a lifetime ago. "Highside" meant for everyone to move to the downstream side of the raft so it would be less likely to be sucked under or flipped.

We moved quickly but not quick enough. Several of us were thrown into the river. Including me.

When I broke the surface, I could see the capsized raft and several fellow rafters about twenty yards upstream. Before I knew it, I cut my leg just below the knee on the sharp edge of a rock. The bad gash in the cold water caused severe pain, and I impulsively grabbed at my wound. Then I remembered. *Keep your toes up and pointed downstream if you find yourself in the water,* our guide had told us. *That way you're less likely to get your foot caught and be pulled under the current.*

As I started to lift my legs and turn around, my head smashed into a boulder. Dazed but still conscious thanks to the helmet I wore, I continued downstream—bouncing uncontrollably like a ball in a giant pinball machine.

I was able to keep my head up but I was tiring quickly. My head was throbbing, my leg was bleeding—and I was in trouble. One thing I'd learned on our many visits to Colorado—sometimes people drown on the rivers, on trips just like ours.

"Jesus, help me!" I called out in desperate fear.

Suddenly, I collided with another log, which stopped me. It was wedged between the rocks just under the surface. One end was near the shore, and in that hopeful moment I thought I might reach safety.

The water pressed cruelly against my back and it took all my strength to push myself up.

Inch by inch, I began to slide along the log. One foot . . . two.

By this time my arms were burning and starting to shake; then I lost my balance. The strong current thrust me headlong into the rapids.

Tumbling, I momentarily lost my bearings and sank in the white, churning water. Instinctively, I tried to paddle upward, but failed to reach the life-giving air. My lungs burned and I soon felt they would burst. What must have been only seconds seemed like hours.

"Lord Jesus . . ."

Darkness closed in and I spun out of consciousness, no longer aware of being swept downstream.

"Connie . . ." Somewhere far away, I heard someone call my name.

"Connie . . ." There it was again—closer this time but not urgent—more like a gentle wakeup call.

I felt strong hands under my arms, pulling me out of the water. I coughed, then opened my eyes. Everything was blurry. Even with repeated blinking, all I could see was a man's white clothing. As he pulled me to a large flat boulder just above the river, I felt his long hair brush against me—but I never saw his face.

"You'll be okay now," he said. "Just relax."

I opened my mouth to thank him but nothing came out. Exhausted, I fell asleep.

The next thing I knew, I heard Tim calling my name. I awakened to see everyone from the raft standing over me.

"Are you okay?" Tim asked, helping me sit up. "That's a nasty gash."

"Well, my head hurts the most. I hit it pretty hard . . . but otherwise I think I'm all right."

Our guide checked my eyes with his flashlight.

"You may have a concussion so you better see a doctor ASAP—but your leg's not as bad as it looks." He took some bandages from the first-aid kit. "Good thing you pulled yourself out when you did. The rapids below here could be deadly without a raft."

"The ones I just came down were bad enough, thank you . . . and I didn't pull myself out. Someone else did."

Everyone looked puzzled, so I told them what happened.

Our guide stopped unrolling gauze and scowled at me.

"This area is nearly impossible to reach except by raft," he said, "and we're the only company currently holding permits for this section of the river. You were either dreaming or that hit on your head is worse than I thought."

My eyes met Tim's—his wry smile told me he believed me—then he turned away.

"That was no dream. I would have drowned if he hadn't pulled me out. . . . I wonder how he knew my name?"

Tim was on one knee now, examining the ground several feet from where I sat.

"I know," he said, barely audible above the sound of the rapids.

"Know what, Dad?" asked Tim Jr. as he ran to his father. Tim held out his arm, stopping him.

"Watch your step, son." He looked back toward the group. "What I said was I know who rescued Connie and how He knew her name."

There was a buzz from the group as they moved toward Tim.

"Watch your step," he repeated. The group peered over Tim Jr.'s shoulders at the rocky ground. There, in the soft earth between the rocks, was a large partial print of a bare foot.

"What do you make of that?" Tim asked.

The guide knelt and gently touched the impression.

"It's fresh—and appears to be human—but who in their right mind would be out here in their bare feet?"

Tim's knowing smile caught our guide off guard—his eyes widened in disbelief. Standing up, Tim stepped to my side.

"Sweetheart, I think you'll want to see this."

I might have been imagining it, but the soft earth felt warm to my fingertips. I knew instantly why Tim was smiling. Perhaps the print by itself meant little—but it was all the proof we needed.

The doctor said I was fortunate to have only a mild concussion and prescribed rest for two to three weeks. That gave me time to reflect.

I should have drowned. Never will I forget the feeling of not being able to breathe. No longer do I take air for granted. Thank God He sent His angel to my rescue.

But why me?

Before long, God showed me. He has a plan. He rescued me so I can help rescue others. That's His plan for me . . . for all of us, really.

Our family still spends a great deal of time outdoors, but now we have a deeper and more balanced outlook. We're not here just for our families or our own pleasure. As long as we have the breath of life, we're here to touch other lives too— especially one-on-one. Sometimes I even tell them this story.

Angels are real, but not everyone has knowingly encountered one. Each of us comes across people every day who need an angel. Though I may not *be* a heavenly angel, by God's grace I can certainly *act* like one.

The Tall Visitor

INGRID SHELTON

It was Christmas Eve, but I was not aware of that special day. Lying in a hospital bed in Germany, I'd hovered between life and death for two days.

As refugees after World War II fleeing the Communist regime, my mother, sister, and I had tried to get across the border from East to West Germany. After two nights, we were successful and, on the West German side, we met with Red Cross workers. They placed us with a farm family in a north German village.

Sick from malnutrition and from walking across the border that cold fall night, I developed pleurisy and pneumonia shortly after arriving at our destination. So I was rushed to a city hospital in Oldenburg some miles away.

Now I lay unconscious in bed, my body wracked with

fever. The doctor held out no hope of my recovery. Somehow the doctor had connected with neighbors of the farm family by phone, asking them to let my mother know I would not survive the night.

I did not realize how severe my illness was. Earlier that day, I had awakened briefly when I had heard a Christmas carol sung somewhere down the hall. But then I had lapsed again into unconsciousness.

During the night I woke suddenly. A tall, gangly man stood by my bed extending his hand toward me. Even though I did not know him, without question I immediately jumped up and stood next to him. Somehow I knew he had something to do with death.

Up to that time I had been terrified of death. I'd heard of dead people appearing to taunt the living, and I didn't know what would happen to me if I died. I was only ten years old and did not want to think about death.

But as I went to the man, I did not experience any type of emotion. I was neither afraid nor sad.

That tall man took me by the hand, and we moved toward the wall. Yet there didn't seem to be a wall. We floated through at least two more rooms and hallways as if the thick walls did not exist until we arrived at a courtyard outside. That courtyard was surrounded by three hospital wings four stories high. Still barefoot and clad in my hospital gown, I did not feel the cold even though snow and frost blanketed the ground.

Suddenly, we heard an authoritative voice coming from somewhere above. The man and I stopped instantly.

"Don't take her. Take him!" the voice commanded. My eyes focused on the second-floor window of one of the wings. I knew that's where the farm family's neighbor boy was hospitalized with diphtheria.

Immediately, the man let go of my hand, grasped my shoulder, and bent my upper body for just a moment. As I bounced back upright, the man disappeared, and I found myself back in my hospital bed.

The next morning, my fever was gone. I was still weak, but I started to recover quickly. My mother rode to the hospital with the neighbor whose son had diphtheria. I was alive and almost well, and my mother was overjoyed.

"Our neighbor's son died suddenly on Christmas Eve night," she told me.

"I know," I said. I was sure the tall man had gone to get the neighbor's son after he let go of me, so the boy's death was not a surprise for me. Yet somehow I could not tell my mother about my Christmas Eve just then. Would she think I had dreamed or hallucinated?

"The neighbors are devastated. They were told the day before that he was recovering," my mother continued. "And you were so sick. I tried to get to the hospital, but no buses or trains were running. And no taxis were available. I stayed up all night worrying about you. I asked our landlord to hitch up the horse to take me to the hospital, but he said the roads were too icy. I am so glad that you have recovered so quickly. It really is a miracle."

"Yes." I nodded, thinking about the Christmas Eve night in the courtyard. Who was the man that came to get me that night? And whose was the authoritative voice we had heard in the courtyard?

I had never heard of God or the Bible.

Just before I was discharged, I took a walk through the hospital and came to a courtyard. I was astonished to recognize it as the one the man had taken me to. Suddenly, I knew beyond a shadow of a doubt that my experience on Christmas Eve had been real, not a hallucination.

Yet from the day the death angel had bent my upper body to the ground, I began to develop scoliosis. Was it to be a reminder of my encounter with spiritual forces? I wondered.

Years went by. Later on in life I finally learned that God was real. Through that hospital experience God had taught me not only that there is life after death, but also that He is in control of the universe. His plan for me was to stay on earth at that time. I realized it was God's voice I had heard in the hospital courtyard on that Christmas Eve night.

Just like God had sent Jesus to die in my place so that I might have eternal life, I feel the young neighbor's son was taken into eternity in my place for reasons I cannot know now. It is a lesson I will always remember. I am grateful that I had another chance at life that Christmas Eve, grateful that God gave me opportunities to share the story of His grace in my life with those around me.

The Divine Mist

CHARLES EARL HARREL

Most people would think that a pastor with thirty years' experience would have witnessed a genuine miracle, but I hadn't, not really.

Oh, I'd seen what some parishioners might call a miracle—like the woman who came down with an illness, probably the flu, but recovered after prayer. Of course, she also stayed home from work, drank plenty of liquids, and had several days of bed rest.

In a similar instance, a man who suffered with severe back pain improved after receiving prayer and visiting his chiropractor.

Most of the events I came across were like that. All good, but situations in which God seemed to work through human means. Nothing is wrong with a good report. Even so, I longed to see or experience a true miracle from above—an unexplainable wonder that left me in awe.

Apparently, God was listening to my thoughts. My encounter with the supernatural realm began unfolding early one Saturday afternoon.

As the pastor of a small Assemblies of God church in Portland, Oregon, I often wore many hats. On that Saturday, I was the worship director looking for a new song for the next day's service. I rushed over to the Christian bookstore conveniently located across the street, hoping someone in the music department would have a suggestion. Unfortunately, the store was slammed that afternoon—all the employees were helping other shoppers.

I selected a CD from the closest display, something about hill songs from Australia, and headed back to Calvary Temple. I was already late for worship practice. As I scanned the list on the back cover, one song grabbed my attention: "I Will Never Be" by Geoff Bullock.

I promptly decided we would use that one for the Sunday services.

Our morning service started on time that Sunday. We were halfway into the worship time when my wife, Laura, who leads the music from her seat at the piano, introduced the new song. The worship team joined her. Our vocalists blended the harmonies well, just as they had in practice.

But something happened that we hadn't experienced during the worship practice.

On our second time through the song, the words pierced my heart as if someone had hammered a nail into it. The pain in my chest lingered—hot, yet not unpleasant. From my seat in the front pew, I glanced around the sanctuary, wondering if others felt the same thing. A few members smiled back at me; everything appeared normal.

Next came the chorus. But I suddenly realized the singing had stopped. I looked toward the piano. Laura had stopped singing. The worship team also fell silent. Several on the platform seemed to have difficulty standing up.

Obviously, something was wrong.

Rushing to the platform to offer my assistance, I noticed a slight glow around the pulpit area, yet I couldn't determine where it was coming from. The temperature in the sanctuary felt as if it had jumped fifteen degrees. I wondered if the janitor had flipped the heat on by mistake.

Then I saw it: up high, a fog-like mist.

The sanctuary looked like a smoke-filled room, but the smoke was coming down instead of rising. Laura kept playing the song, silently mouthing the words from the chorus. Her eyes remained closed.

Charlie, our drummer, broke into a blazing solo on his drums—I didn't know he could play that well—then he stopped and sat still. Eddie continued to pick slowly on lead guitar, while the other guitarists appeared as though they had forgotten the chords. The bass player just held his instrument and sat quietly on the steps. Our vocalists, Peggy and Sylvia, were kneeling with their faces on the floor, microphones lying beside them.

I felt a tug behind my knees, like a riptide or swift current in a river. I could see why standing was difficult. People throughout the sanctuary were kneeling or bowing down; several lay prostrate on the floor. They looked as though they were glued to the carpet. I couldn't stand either; an unseen force knocked me to the floor.

As I pondered the words of the song, I heard giggles. Several children were laughing as they looked up at the ceiling, their eyes moving right to left, then back again. I wondered what they were watching. Later, one of them told me he saw an outline of a hand waving slowly over the altar area. Several adult members witnessed the same thing. All I observed was the misty smoke, but I believed their testimony because they were people of integrity, including my wife, Laura. All these unexplainable events or signs were just the prelude—more were on the way.

The morning service never really ended; it continued throughout the afternoon. When I finally got off the floor, I talked with several parishioners. Although it was late, no one was in a hurry to leave. One man had no more pain in his back. A condition he had suffered with for years was gone, instantly, yet no one had prayed for him. A couple in a failing marriage had somehow fallen in love again. One smiling, the other in tears, they went home—divorce no longer an option. The Holy Spirit used a simple song to release a miracle and accomplish what years of counseling could not.

I didn't recognize the last person I talked with. He told me he heard people singing as he walked down a nearby street. The words cut deeply into his heart, and the music compelled him to enter the church. That's when he saw the divine mist and felt a warming presence. He dropped to the floor and wept for hours. When this man, Carl, got up, his life had changed; he would never abuse drugs again. There were other testimonies—all compelling, all miraculous.

Certain songs become popular, and we enjoy singing or listening to them. Once in a while, though, a song touches heaven. The song turns into a fiery prayer for something more, and God answers back, pouring out miracle after miracle.

And when God starts pouring out the miracles, well, we are never the same again.

The Evil Creatures Who Fizzled

ANGIE REEDY

I hope I'm never closer to hell than I was that June day. Fire-breathing, nostril-flaring, red-eyed dragons greeted us when we opened the door to the warehouse far up the Amazon River. Even though I knew these contraptions were man-made, evil radiated around our band of prayer warriors, creating chills deep in my soul.

Our guide proudly showed us the mechanics of each beast's movements and the special effects the monsters could perform.

I couldn't understand a word of his quick-firing Portuguese, but his passion for the creations didn't need translation. He told us about the hundreds of hours he and his teammates sacrificed to create the lifelike monsters. And he affirmed his belief that his red team's creatures would triumph over the blue team's equally hellish designs.

Our little group had first traveled to Brazil to spend time with our missionary relatives. Besides encouraging them and praying over their ministry, we were to complete work projects around their church.

We expected a safe, comfortable visit, but God had other plans. Our small missionary entourage made the arduous line boat journey up the Amazon to Parintins just in time to pray against the town's annual carnival-esque *Festa do Boi* (Festival of the Bull).

Bulls and celebrations don't inherently prompt prayers for confusion and the intervention of good. But people came from surrounding villages and even faraway European countries to participate in the festival. And the town's church always saw destructive effects. The festival generated a renewed interest in the work of demonic spirits in that jungle society.

For more than thirty years, the red and blue teams had prepared to wow the crowds and claim victory through an annual competition. This stemmed from a folk story about a pregnant slave woman who persuaded her husband to bring her the tongue of a bull to eat. After killing the master's best bull, the loyal husband received a death sentence until his wife employed a witch doctor to resurrect the bull, thus saving her husband.

In honor of this legend, two families annually create bulls and parade them around the city. A singer accompanies each bull during its tour, proclaiming its dominance over the bull of the other family. Over the years the annual unveiling of the bulls on the third day has grown into a passionate event that attracts thousands of revelers.

We arrived during the height of their preparations. Because the celebration hinders the spiritual work of the local church so much, they asked us to leave our church building-repair projects and go pray against the festival.

So we traded our paintbrushes and hammers for Bibles and comfy shoes. We walked around the bull-shaped stadium where events would be held twice every day. As we walked, we prayed for God's presence to overcome the darkness of the coming events.

During that week we walked.

We prayed.

We asked God to confuse the plans and send rain on the days of the event.

We pled for disagreement among the organizers and malfunction of all things technological.

As the days passed, the enemy knocked out our team members one by one. Sickness and hives plagued our group, finally leaving six of our original fourteen prayer warriors marching around the stadium. Rather than becoming discouraged, our strength grew as we recognized the reality of the battle we fought.

In the middle of our prayers against the event, the red team invited us to enter their sacred storehouse of preparation. We quickly accepted the opportunity to see what exactly our prayers aimed against, and that's when I felt like I'd stepped into an annex of hell.

The inside of the building reminded me of a Hollywood movie set. The sophisticated animation and special effects produced from a sleepy jungle town amazed me.

After seeing the incredible work of the red team, we prayed even harder in our remaining days for God to glorify himself and weaken the grip the enemy had over the town.

At our appointed time, even as partiers streamed into the town, we boarded the commercial line boat, slung our hammocks around the top deck, and left the increasing rise of party fever, returning to the church and missionaries we'd come to visit in the first place. A week later we began our journey out of the Brazilian sauna.

But God had more for us.

I've often prayed for God's intervention over unseen spiritual forces, yet rarely do I get to see His tangible answer. But in this situation, we did hear about God's answer to our prayers.

On our flight home from Manaus to Miami, my sister Becky sat next to an American special effects producer returning from the *Festa do Boi*. He began telling her why he would never return to work on this project in the Amazon again. Although he had traveled to Brazil hoping to help the red team in a small river town, everything his crew touched backfired. Despite attempts to create an incredible display highlighted with special effects sure to wow even the soberest celebrators, nothing seemed to work.

Becky's seatmate described his experience in Parintins as absolutely miserable.

It rained almost every day!

When they attempted to raise the naked woman float to her full height, she crumbled to dust on the ground.

A simple telephone wire caught the largest, most demonic looking creature with eerie glowing eyes, and he burned down before being able to breathe any fire out of his nostrils.

Fireworks ordered to arrive in time for the big stadium display never came.

Even though he specifically requested an air-conditioned room, this producer sweltered in a stuffy room without cooled air.

I sympathize with anyone sleeping in the sweltering heat of that jungle town on the equator without air-conditioning, but I rejoice over the way God frustrated the plans exactly as we asked. Just one man's experience gave us a peek into the creativity God used to answer our prayers.

An evil creature catching on a utility line and burning to the ground?

We couldn't have conceived such a creative way to stomp on the darkness covering the town.

God's orchestration of Becky's seatmate encouraged our short-term missionary group with a solid faith in prayer. We could have received emails reporting the news from our Parintins missionary relatives. We could have scoured the Internet looking for news about that year's festivities. But God provided abundantly beyond what we could ask or imagine.

He spoke personally to us.

Maybe He could hardly contain His excitement over the victories accomplished in the town, so He directly shared the results with us.

Maybe He knew we needed to know specific details of those answered prayers to solidify our faith.

Maybe He longed for us to catch a glimpse of His glorious creativity in defeating the enemy.

Or maybe He simply knew His children needed to see a miracle.

A New and Radiant Heart

LINDA JETT

"You and your friend were related in a past life in Egypt," the masculine voice announced at my private "reading." The voice droned on, filling in details that explained centuries of my soul's existence. Finally, at the end of the reading, the female pastor of this small country church emerged from her trance to bid me good-bye in her normal voice.

When I told the results to my housemate, she exclaimed, "I knew we had a connection that couldn't be explained by the fact that we work for the same employer!"

I didn't share her enthusiasm. Something didn't feel right about this new revelation. I'd recently walked away from my marriage and my three-year-old daughter. I felt I had failed at traditional values, so I liked the security offered by familiar old hymns and Bible passages when I visited my housemate's place of worship. But deep down I knew the Bible did not support the past-lives theory the pastor and others in this church held.

Meanwhile, two hundred miles away, my mother cried her heart out to God. She could not understand why her only child, an intelligent college graduate, had left her marriage, her child, and the belief system in which she'd been raised. Whether locked in her semi-dark bedroom, or out in the sunshine among her flower gardens, my mother faithfully prayed for me day after day.

Empowered by God's wisdom, she and my father never distanced themselves from my husband or took sides. They stayed in touch with their only grandchild, no matter how much pain it brought. They also reached out to me, trying to accept me right where I was, even when they couldn't understand the reasons for my choices.

I couldn't explain how the growing hurts, disappointments, and misunderstandings had culminated in an outbreak of violence that finally destroyed my marriage. So I severed communication with my mom and dad. In their place I tried to build a new family of free thinkers.

I relied on these new friends for my direction, my peace, and my security. Together we drank late into the night, worked at the same company during the day, and took off for extended hikes and adventures on the weekends. At first I felt empowered—no longer encumbered by marriage, parenthood, or trying to please my parents.

Advanced yoga sessions ended with group meditations. As humming sounds filled our exercise space, I sensed a shift in the unseen world around me. I felt the prickly edge of fear warning me that this "peace" was really an illusion.

"Altered states of consciousness" read the community college class description. It sounded invigorating. *Why not?*

I persuaded another roommate, a former Wiccan, to attend the sessions with me. We warmed to the ideas of Transcendental Meditation and Hare Krishna. Communal living seemed like a happy solution to the loneliness I felt.

Eventually my searching led to another job. That led to the excitement of newly formed illicit relationships. One was with a shaman who held a highly respected position at the company where I worked. He introduced me to concepts like astral projection. Although scintillating at first, the myriad ideas and experiences did not bring the peace and security I longed for, but rather a deep mistrust in surface appearances.

Drugs and alcohol numbed my pain. But one night fear devoured a part of my fragile stability. It rode in on the form of a dog, a stray Great Dane that had wandered into our lives and into our country house. One night the dog's image shifted shapes in my dreams. Or was I having a drug-induced hallucination? He grew into a terrifying monster waiting to attack me.

The dream left an indescribable terror in my heart.

More fear came several years later when I faced my own mortality through a debilitating blood disease. Reaching the end of the world's resources and myself, I struggled for freedom from the bonds of fear and darkness. I moved out of a communal living situation and began pouring my heart out to the God I'd known since early childhood.

"I've made a mess of this whole thing," I sobbed as I jogged around the local school track in darkness and then returned to the townhouse where I now lived alone.

"God, it's okay if you take my life. I'm sorry for what I've done." Tears began their cleansing process as I surrendered again and again.

Finally the doctors removed my spleen. As my body recuperated, God began rebuilding my inner and outer life on a firmer foundation based on His truth. I began attending a church that accurately preached from the Bible. I hungered for His Word and began studying in earnest, both alone and in a Bible study.

At church I eventually met a man who also desired to live God's Word in a practical, everyday way. We married a few months later.

Many years after that, the church offered a series on healing prayer. As a massage therapist, I gravitated toward anything that might help my hurting clients. But first I needed to experience deeper inner healing myself. I studied the Bible, prayed fervently with other believers, admitted my past involvement with occult practices, and asked the Lord to remove any traces of influence those encounters might have left in my own mind and belief system.

Then I participated in a spiritual retreat.

Toward the end of the sessions, I sat quietly in a church pew, planning to meditate on God's Word, when Christ suddenly stood before me. As His eyes of love penetrated my soul, He reached into my chest and withdrew my heart.

Blackened, hardened, it was not beating as He cupped it in His hands. Then He gently breathed new life into it. Radiating with iridescence, it began beating. He returned it to my chest and announced, "I have given you a new name."

When the vision ended, I looked up to see if anyone else had witnessed this very intimate moment. No one appeared to have noticed. But all the way home I shouted, "God is my Father! He loves me just as I am. He delights over me with singing. He has given me a new name!" Words could not contain the joy I felt.

Deep within, I know that I could not have left my former life of deception, bondage, and fear if it hadn't been for God's power unleashed by my mother's faithful prayers, day after day, year after year.

After thirty-two years of marriage, the birth of a son, a restored relationship with my daughter, and the birth of three grandchildren, I look forward to the day when I enter heaven and can thank Mom for her faithfulness in battling for me in the unseen realms.

Determined prayer warriors united with God can see miracles happen!

I know; I am proof.

Backseat Angels

SALLY EDWARDS DANLEY

S ally, I like your collection of angel statues. Have you ever seen a real angel?"

My friend Marcia asked that question on her first visit to my home many years ago. She was standing in front of the little cabinet one of my sons had given me for Christmas. With its glass front, I felt that was a good place to put the cute little angel gifts that I'd received.

"No, Marcia, I haven't, but I'm fascinated with the stories about them," I responded.

I had started to receive Christian magazines that included stories about angel sightings, and I loved reading them. I'd also heard preaching and read Bible verses referring to angels. Knowing my intrigue, my three teenagers and others would occasionally give me angel statues or clothes with angel artwork.

For the most part, I found it fun to think that angels might be real. The more stories I read, the more I hoped to someday see one. But I felt it was not likely.

Then my daughter turned my world upside down.

When Jeannie was a senior in high school, she was dating a handsome schoolmate.

Needless to say, I was upset when she joyfully informed me I was going to be a grandmother. I had worked so hard to try to instill in her the importance of maintaining her virginity until marriage. She told me on my thirty-ninth birthday, thinking it would make me happy. It didn't.

Her boyfriend was not happy either. He was not ready for marriage, much less for being a dad. But Jeannie thought surely he'd come around and they'd have a wedding before the baby came. When they both graduated from high school a few months later, he joined the Marines and left town.

Jeannie was upset and surprised. She didn't hear from him again for ten years.

My own marriage had fallen apart, and as a single mother I was the sole support of my family. My job did not bring in a large income, but I was able to provide a home for Jeannie and my sons, Patrick, a junior, and Scott, a sophomore in high school.

Now I was feeling financially responsible for the baby. I convinced Jeannie it would be best if she placed the child for adoption. We arranged for an appointment with an agency that handled such matters. But Jeannie rarely smiled after we made that date.

The week before our appointment, one evening when I came home from work, Jeannie asked me to sit down and talk with her. I'd planned to do that anyway, since I'd experienced something important earlier that day.

"Mama," she said, "I know it doesn't make sense, but I really felt God was telling me today that we should keep the baby."

I was only slightly surprised. With a soft smile I told her, "God told me the very same thing today, Jeannie."

We looked at each other with a sense of awe and joy as tears trickled down our cheeks. How could we fight that nudging both of us felt at the same time?

I didn't know how on earth I'd pay for the added expense of another child, yet I felt a peace that it would all be taken care of.

Of course, as girls do, we both got excited about getting things together for the baby. We didn't know if the child would be a boy or girl, but secretly we both hoped for a little girl. And we shopped for blankets and shirts with angels on them.

It was a beautiful October day when Jeannie's daughter, Shawna, was born. I was beside her and joyously watched my first grandchild being delivered. I felt it was a miracle. All my fears and concerns faded. No longer did I care if I was too young to be a grandmother. All worries about financing the baby disappeared. I only felt in awe of this precious little angel.

After Jeannie was taken to a hospital room to rest, I left for my job as bookkeeper and secretary at a small laboratory. Announcing the birth of my grandchild was fun. After catching up on paper work and phone calls, I stepped outside to catch my breath and bask in the bright sunshine.

Sitting on those small cement steps, I looked up at the clear blue sky. My heart was full of gratitude.

"Thank you, Lord," I said out loud. That memorable moment is still clear. I felt such awe. I had delivered three babies of my own but had never seen one born.

A few weeks later, Jeannie returned to her job at a fast-food place. She set her schedule to work evenings so her brothers could help care for the baby. They both worked after school too, but they arranged their schedules to be sure one of them would always be there for baby Shawna until I got home from work.

That went well for a few months, and then Jeannie decided she needed to move out on her own. I hated that and argued against it. I'd gotten used to having little Shawna around and loved her so much. Naturally, I felt responsible for her. But part of me knew I had to relinquish that responsibility to Shawna's mom.

We helped Jeannie and the baby move into an apartment about twenty minutes from our home. Her boss arranged for her to transfer to a shop nearer her new place. She worked full time and began leaving the baby in day care.

A few months later, Jeannie called and said, "Mama, Friday evening I'm going to take Shawna to Oklahoma City so she can meet her four great-grandparents."

I was hurt that I hadn't been invited and struggled to accept that my daughter was an adult now, so I had to respect her decisions. But I was concerned about her making that five-hour drive for the first time with a baby.

"I'll go after work so Shawna will be sleeping. I think the traffic will be lighter at night," she said. That made sense. How could I argue? Instead, I softly asked, "Will you at least come by and let me pray over you and the baby before you go?"

"Sure," she said. "I'll be there about ten-fifteen, but I can't stay long."

"I understand," I assured her.

Friday night, she showed up promptly. I'd been watching from the front window so I could meet her outside and avoid wasting time.

Since this was her first trip out of town on her own, Jeannie was excited. As Jeannie had hoped, Shawna was sound asleep.

I wrapped my arms around Jeannie and hugged her firmly. Laying one hand on her and one on her car, I prayed a blessing of safety and protection.

"Lord, I know you'll be with Jeannie and the baby all the way to Granny and Pawpaw's house. I trust you, Lord, to protect them every mile of the way." Then, after a moment of hesitation, I added, "And, Lord, I ask you to please assign angels to guard and protect Jeannie and little Shawna."

She slipped into her car and drove away as I watched. When they neared the end of my short block, I was stunned to see two golden, glowing beings in her backseat. Blinking, I looked again and they were still there.

With a soft smile, I walked inside shaking my head slowly, thinking it was surely my imagination. Angels don't really exist. Do they?

But I went to bed and right to sleep without another concern for my girls. I slept soundly and awoke feeling a gentle peace Saturday morning. I was amazed I'd gone right to sleep without a moment of worry. That was very unusual for me.

Somehow I knew they were safely in Oklahoma City at the home of my former in-laws. Since they were probably sleeping in, I didn't want to call to make sure they'd arrived safely. But about 8:00 a.m. my phone rang.

Jeannie was on the line to tell me they had a safe, uneventful trip and made good time. She hesitated and then said, "And Mama, I know this sounds crazy, but I swear it's the truth. Mama, there were two glowing gold angels riding in the backseat all the way. They never said a word. They were just there and disappeared when I pulled into Granny's driveway."

I hadn't said a word to her about what I had seen as she drove away.

That day we both learned angels are real.

The Trees Are Real Again

Joe Murphy

The trees didn't look real.

I thought I could pass my hands right through them, they were so ephemeral. That's what the world looked like to me at age nineteen, but I didn't consider why my perceptions had so changed. My mind was focused on other things and I was caught up in myself.

Each time I took a dose of LSD or another drug, I would experience something worse. I kept doing it, wanting to get past those bad trips and get back to what I thought was a pure form of consciousness.

I thought I had experienced God.

God became greatly important to me when my attempt to find some sense of fulfillment in a relationship with a girl appeared to be futile. I knew I was seeking to resolve some inner need, and I had tried for years to establish a satisfying emotional connection with girls I cared for.

It all became a tangled mess. I feared that the one girl I really cared for in high school was not going to stick with me once we left for college. Rather than feel that pain, I broke up with her to get it over with and pushed her out of my mind. In college I struck up a number of relationships only to have them end for this or that reason without learning anything useful about myself.

After one particularly frustrating encounter, I mentally detached from it all and thought that I was misplacing my hopes.

What I really want is God, and I'm looking in the wrong place, I decided. So I set off in pursuit of Him.

Finding God, however, turned into a terrifying journey. For an anthropology class paper, I did some research in the Library of Congress's endless collection of books. I convinced myself that through psychedelic drug use, I could experience God in the same way Christian mystics had experienced Him. So I promptly obtained three times the standard dose of LSD and took it.

The resulting experience was exactly like what I read: absorption of my consciousness into white light.

Yep. God.

The problem was, when the drugs wore off, God was gone.

That's problematic for a Being who is by definition omnipresent—but the god I was pursuing at that point definitely wasn't that. The god I was after was elusive but greatly rewarding. If you had the skill, perseverance, and dedication to train your consciousness—or had the drugs to train your consciousness for you—you could have the God consciousness, resolving all inner needs and problems.

Of course, you lost personal distinction as well, your own sense of being a unique person, but I was not considering that then.

A practical plan, it seemed, was to take more drugs and start to train my consciousness. The drugs gave me a present leg up, while Buddhist meditation promised eventual nirvana. I spent a summer in London, practicing both. That cocktail had a kick that I didn't expect. Having cut my long hair, which I loved, toward achieving the Buddhist goal of selflessness, I arrived alone in a foreign country almost fully shaved at a time when others of my generation wore very long hair.

By the end of the summer, I was disconnected and distant, lonely and alienated. My friends back at college thought I had gotten weird and avoided me. My drug trips became intense and frightening.

One trip was particularly disturbing. The next morning, I picked up a copy of Dante's *Inferno*, which I'd never read, and found descriptions of what I had seen the night before—a dragon indicating with his tail which level of hell a person was condemned to!

The really terrifying thing is that it fit me, and I knew it. I saw angels and demons on these trips, and at the edges of my awareness, the trees were losing solidity.

A few months later, on Christmas vacation, a friend told me about the spiritual journey of another mutual friend. "John is a Jesus freak," he said.

Thinking that odd but interesting, we decided to go razz our old high school friend John and tell him Jesus had sent us.

John was never serious in school and was always in trouble. As soon as we met him that day, we saw the change in him. He had a new mantle of thoughtfulness. We lost our sense of mischief right away and plied him with questions, attempting to disabuse him of his new faith. The mere idea that Jesus alone was the path to salvation and eternal life seemed ludicrous to us. John quoted things Jesus said and we parted after about an hour's conversation.

Jesus' words stayed with me and disturbed me, though. I began reading the New Testament. I didn't understand it all, but what I did understand bothered me, because Jesus said things that didn't fit my worldview. The Eastern religions and the "all roads lead to the same God" mystics presented Him quite differently.

In the Bible He claimed to be uniquely God and said only through Him could someone come to know God: "I am the way and the truth and the life. No one comes to the Father except through me" (John 14:6). I realized that whatever Jesus was talking about wasn't what Buddhists and others were talking about. For the first time, I really wanted God, because I wanted Jesus.

Then something occurred that I can't explain. One night after falling asleep, I woke to an incredible shaking and shuddering, as if I were being hurtled through space like an airplane. Everything was pitch black, except for twinkling white or yellow and red lights in the distance directly ahead of me.

"Who is there to help me?" I screamed. The voice was mine but sounded like someone else at the same time.

"Jesus," another voice answered.

My shaking stopped. Then I felt myself very gently lifted. I was relaxed and at peace instead of feeling the terror I had just experienced. Soon I saw myself enter the basement of our house, then rise successively through the first and second floor, and enter my body, which was lying on my bed.

I heard my mother, asleep in the next room, call my name. I tried to answer and couldn't. It took a few moments for me to become acclimated to my body. Finally, I was in completely normal consciousness.

"What?" I opened my mouth and answered my mother out loud.

That just made me laugh; she was sound asleep! I turned over, still quite at peace, and soon fell sound asleep.

What, precisely, did I experience? An out-of-body experi- ence? A dream? Dying in my sleep? A drug flashback?

Who knows?

I only know I now had a greater confidence that Jesus was who He said He was. But my life did not yet change.

I still plodded on using drugs, no more conscious of God in my daily life than before. The idea of Jesus gripped me, but it was just an idea until I read Fyodor Dostoevsky's *The Idiot*. The prince in the story is a Christ figure, and the concepts of innocence and sin in the story jogged my memory. As a four-year-old boy, I had stolen a chocolate lollipop from a grocery store in my hometown. I knew it was wrong, but when my mother told me I couldn't have it and turned her back, I took it and hid it under the seat in the car.

As I sat there with the book in my lap, I realized I was a sinner. It wasn't bad karma or anything else. I knew right from wrong, and I chose wrong. I alone was responsible for my actions.

Reading that novel, I understood who the idiot is: me. Of all the sins I had committed after that time—hurting so many people and wrecking so many relationships—this first sin showed me the principle at work in all the others.

I thought God was distant and a force or state of being to be obtained. No, He is a person, as I am a person made like Him, and from the very beginning of my ability to choose, I had offended Him.

As soon as I admitted to Him that night that I was a sinner and asked His forgiveness through Jesus Christ, He made me know His forgiveness and overwhelmed me with His presence.

The words I used to describe it then, I later came to learn were used by Jesus to describe God's Holy Spirit inside us: a river that is alive, overflowing within us (John 7:38).

God is not distant; I had distanced myself. I hadn't been pursuing God; I had been running away. Jesus is not only the way back, but He had sent me to visit our friend John! He had found me.

The next morning, I was completely and uniquely myself, yet aware of God everywhere. In my perception, the world that God made was now real and good, as it has always been. The trees were solid again.

Peril at the Cut River Bridge

PATRICIA L. STEBELTON

A quick glance out the kitchen window told me it would be an overcast day, but that was no surprise. This was Michigan, surrounded on three sides by large masses of water, the Great Lakes.

I reminded myself that the weather bureau predicted sunshine for the next few days. The blush of fall hues on the tips of our maple trees in Chelsea was a promise of the blaze of color they would be in less than two weeks. But I wasn't waiting . . . in twenty-four hours my husband and I were headed to the Upper Peninsula—known by Michiganders as "God's country." There, the fall color would be in full array, and we were rushing to embrace it.

I love fall. It's my chance each year to see the Master Creator in living action . . . in the very process of painting a wild, splashy landscape that never fails to take my breath away. Knowing this, my husband arranges for a few days each year when we can dash to the north for the great show—our special getaway. My excitement was mounting by the hour.

As we crossed the magnificent Mackinac Bridge, I was aware of the powerful wind sway beneath us. Eagerly, I peered down on the straits between the Lower and Upper Peninsulas, where the moody blue-gray of the sky reflected in the wave swells as the rough water from Lake Huron collided with Lake Michigan in a contest of wills.

I gazed across to Mackinac Island, watching the rooster tails of fast-paced ferries race tourists to the island, and sailboats keeled heavily on their sides. Soon the ferries would be stored and the Victorian island left to its lonely, secluded winter.

Holding the sight in my mind to bring up later in leisurely moments, I faced forward, expectant of the radiant beauty awaiting us on the other side of the bridge.

On the Upper Peninsula, towering pine trees lined the curving highway leading to the Cut River Bridge, where the high ridges sweeping into the bottom of the gorge would be a solid blanket of raging color. The coolness of morning mixed with the rising sun coated the hillsides with a muted mist—almost a fog.

My husband, Dick, pulled our '81 Omni off the road on the near side of the two-lane Cut River Bridge and parked. I wanted to see the entire gorge in the brightness of full sunlight and suggested we hike the winding trail that eventually led to the edge of Lake Michigan. I hoped the mist might burn off by the time we returned to the top.

The downward graveled trail was caked with mud from the moisture in the air, and the rotting vegetation was pungent in our nostrils as we stepped carefully, trying not to slide to the bottom of the gorge.

We heard the waves roar, slapping against the shoreline as we came to the end of the trail. The wind rippled loudly through the poplar trees, their leaves rustling all around us. Our hair flung across our faces and into our eyes as spray from a cold, wayward wave tingled our cheeks. It was exhilarating!

"Caw! Caw!" The seagulls demanded we give them food as their wings beat the air above our heads. I rummaged my pockets for the crushed crackers in cellophane packages. But as I looked at the skies, I felt a growing sense of discouragement. The mist was not burning off. The clouds were merging into a solid gray overcast day.

I knew the brilliant yellows, golds, and reds of the maple trees would be dulled without direct sun to illuminate them.

My planned holiday lacked luster, like the scenery—it was simply a day like any other.

My husband and I walked hand and hand up the steep trail to the top level and paused to survey the soft beauty of the hillside cliffs. I sighed—maybe next year I would view this scene in all its sparkling delight.

Climbing into our blue Omni, we strapped our seat belts around us and looked ahead at the deserted two-lane bridge shrouded partly in fog. It would carry us across the Cut River Gorge.

Dick turned the ignition while I twisted in my seat to put on my jacket. The weather felt suddenly chilly. I thought briefly of our growing family at home and experienced an unexpected sharp pang of missing them.

Dick craned his neck to check oncoming traffic in the right lane we would merge into. There were no cars, so his foot pressed down on the accelerator, then abruptly stopped.

My head jerked. I stared at him, suddenly surrounded by a whishing noise and loud vibration shaking our little car. A huge semi-truck whizzed by our vehicle on the left, missing us by inches. A second later, we felt the suction of its aftermath and wet spray rising from the concrete.

My husband's face paled and he lifted his hands from the steering wheel. We shook as we both realized how close we'd come to death.

"What happened?" I cried, my throat dry with fear.

"I—I was ready to pull out—my foot was on the gas . . . but I couldn't move! I was held in place!"

His breathing was irregular.

"It was just as if *someone* held me back!"

I continued to stare, trying to understand.

"Where did that truck come from? He was on the wrong side of the road—flying!"

Dick licked his lips. "He wasn't there when I started. It's a two-lane bridge. I figured I had nothing to worry about from the opposite direction, so I checked behind us. That semi-truck must have passed another car on the bridge."

"Is that legal?"

"It wouldn't have mattered whether it was legal or not if I'd pulled into that lane. That semi would have hit us *head on.*" He turned to look at me in horror. "There wouldn't have been *anything* left of us!"

My hands were shaking. It was the first time I realized how small our car was, compared with the semi we'd narrowly missed. Both of us sat in silence for several minutes, too nervous to move.

"Thank you, Jesus," Dick finally prayed. His words were barely a whisper.

I echoed his prayer. Suddenly, it no longer mattered if the

sun was shining on the hillside across the gorge. My husband and I were sitting in our little car more alive than we'd been all day. Another Presence had been with us in our vehicle. There was no doubt in our minds that God's protective Spirit was with us. Was it a guardian angel holding Dick back from pulling out on the highway?

While we could only speculate, we knew God had been there with us in some form.

A few days later, Dick and I returned to our children and our everyday lives. We went about our daily routines and made plans for the future, more aware than ever that God orders our future and numbers our days. It is up to us to live in a way that glorifies our Lord. Neither my husband nor I will ever take the next day in our life for granted.

Heaven's Soldier

MARIANNA CARPENTER WIECK,
as told to LINDA W. ROOKS

My mother was an evangelist. For eighteen years she traveled the country, speaking in tent meetings and starting new churches.

As she went from state to state, local newspapers touted her as an evangelist God "called from the kitchen to the pulpit." She attracted hundreds of people to her meetings. Reporters said Mrs. A. A. Carpenter's preaching was "powerful" and "under forceful anointing." And they described her as "fearless and dynamic."

The event that led to her call into the ministry, however, was not something any woman would want to face.

I was a curly-haired blonde of seven when it all happened. My brother, Wallace, was nineteen. World War I had just begun, and being a fine, brave, patriotic young man, Wallace enlisted in the Army, as so many others did at that time.

Wallace went off to be a soldier, but before he fought one battle, and after barely trying on his uniform, he was confronted by a private war of his own. Stationed in Iowa City, Iowa, he fell victim to pneumonia. After a week in the Army, my older brother, a fine young man so admired by the people of his hometown of Mount Pleasant, Iowa, died.

Wallace's death devastated my mother. He had been the perfect young man: an outstanding student, active in the local Methodist Church, highly respected in the community, and an attentive son. Every evening after dinner, before picking up his fiancée, Letha, he had brought the car around and took Mother on a ride through town. They rode around the square where friends would wave to her, then they drove up and down the streets of the neighborhood.

She was the envy of every other mother in Mount Pleasant, partly because they had one of the first cars in town, but mostly because she had such a thoughtful son. Mother loved him dearly.

The day after Wallace died was traumatic for my family. My parents and Letha were grief-stricken and decided to drive to Iowa City, where he had died. They arrived late and checked into a hotel for the night. Mother and Letha went to their rooms to go to bed, but Daddy knew he could not sleep, so he decided to sit up alone for a while in another room.

Overcome with grief, my mother wrestled sleeplessly in her bed that night, tossing and turning, crying and praying. Suddenly, she looked up and saw Wallace standing at the foot of her bed. He was leaning on Jesus. He looked radiant.

"Over here everything is love," he said reassuringly. "Everything is love."

Then he was gone.

Mother was amazed at what she'd seen and was filled with a peace she couldn't explain. What did this mean? How could this be? Should she tell the others what she'd experienced?

The next morning when Mother joined my father and Letha for breakfast, she hesitated to mention her vision to them. Surely they would think she was hallucinating. While they were sitting around the breakfast table, Daddy, my rational, realistic, unimaginative father, cleared his throat. He spoke cautiously but resolutely.

"I had the strangest experience last night," he said.

As he spoke, Mother and Letha stared at him in amazement. With his typically calm demeanor, he described seeing Wallace leaning on Jesus and saying, "Over here everything is love. Everything is love."

"Why, I saw the very same thing!" Mother cried.

"So did I!" Letha echoed with a look of wonder on her face.

When they returned home, they told the story to the rest of us. It seemed God in His mercy and love had sent Wallace to comfort his loved ones.

That event catapulted Mother into more encounters with the Lord that year and a close, vibrant relationship with Him. She became a changed woman and felt God calling her to become an evangelist. Shortly afterward, she began traveling around the country, sharing her testimony, helping start churches, and often telling the story of Wallace's appearance to his loved ones after his death. While Wallace never fought a battle as a soldier in the U.S. Army, in the battle over people's souls, Wallace joined with the soldiers of heaven to bring the victory of eternal life to many.

I was only seven then, but it changed my life as well. Whenever I was tempted to doubt, I remembered this story told by three people I knew and trusted. My faith became cemented in the knowledge that heaven is real and that love is what matters most. I knew from the age of seven years old that this is what Jesus came to tell us.

Now as I sit at the doorstep of heaven waiting for the day I, too, shall walk into eternity, I find comfort in the promise of God's all-encompassing and everlasting love that my brother brought from heaven so long ago.

For like the apostle Paul, "I am convinced that neither death nor life, neither angels nor demons, neither the present nor the future, nor any powers, neither height nor depth, nor anything else in all creation, will be able to separate us from the love of God that is in Christ Jesus our Lord" (Romans 8:38–39).

The Heavenly Choir

FRAN COURTNEY-SMITH, as told to
PAT STOCKETT JOHNSTON

The comrades."
The very name struck terror in the hearts of the villagers . . . and in my heart too!

I was the school nurse at the Arthurseat Nazarene Bible College in the Eastern Transvaal, South Africa, just before the apartheid was abolished. I also visited surrounding villages and taught women how to care for their children, make gardens, strain water with a cloth to remove debris, and purify water by adding one drop of household bleach to every liter.

I loved my busy life. Until the comrades entered our world.

The comrades were young African men who likened themselves to communists. They would go through villages and steal whatever they wanted. They also burned down houses.

Then they turned their sites on the old people. Minor infractions led them to accuse many elders of being witches. The old people who were labeled this way were then condemned to death by the terrible method of necklacing—car tires were put over their heads and set on fire. It was a horrible way to die!

Everyone was afraid of the comrades. Then they announced that they wanted to hold meetings in the big tabernacle on the mission station. The Bible college refused to give permission.

The male students became very worried and began to hold prayer meetings late into each night asking for protection and begging the Lord to keep them from being forced to help those who were necklacing.

During those dangerous times, the authorities told me to pack a suitcase and set it by my front door so I'd be ready to leave at a moment's notice. I sent my clinic workers home, as I felt they'd be safer away from the mission station. Soon I was the only white person left on the grounds.

My house was built at the crest of a small hill on the station. Standing outside my front door, I could see a flood of refugees fleeing on the road below. People were carrying bundles and driving donkey carts and old trucks, or pushing wheelbarrows, or using whatever they could to carry their belongings and flee the violence.

I stared at my lovely garden, my chickens, and my dog, and became frightened. What would happen to them and to me if the comrades arrived?

"I know you are with me and will never leave me," I told the Lord. "But I'm so afraid. I need something more than I've ever had before to cope."

Dusk was approaching, so I went inside and shut and locked the door.

Soon, though, my dog began pacing the floor and growling at the door and window. I decided to play some of the good old hymns on my tape recorder. The music seemed to hit me on the head and relax every muscle in my exhausted body. I went to bed.

About three in the morning I vaguely heard my dog stir. Then he jumped up and sat up straight on my bed.

Ah. Here come the comrades, I thought. *I need to put on my glasses so I can see what's going on.*

I heard a noise.

Whatever is that? Music? No, it can't be. Maybe it's coming from down on the road. A group making their way home after drinking beer.

Then I remembered. Terrified people don't sing. They move as quickly and quietly as possible. The music got louder. I couldn't understand the words, so I knew the language wasn't Shangaan, Zulu, or Sotho.

Oh. Maybe the Venda student is teaching everyone a song in his language. Or the male students had such a good prayer meeting they are going to tell the girls about it.

I quickly realized this would not be happening at three in the morning. So I went to my big office window and stared at the beautiful full moon shining over the landscape. Every leaf on the banana and avocado trees shimmered in the moonlight. It was so bright you could have read a newspaper outside. I couldn't see a soul.

All the time, the sound of the music came closer and closer. It was a magnificent choir of African male voices, the rich basses, baritones, and tenors singing what felt like a song of praise in a language I didn't know. I didn't understand where the music was coming from.

I searched the area outside my window. No shadows

darkened the path outside. No footprints marred the sand that had been blown clean by the wind earlier in the evening. No one in sight.

Finally, the music moved away over the hill. I slipped back into bed and slept more deeply than I had for many nights. The next morning I was up early and went to check on my neighbors down the road. The two toddlers were sitting in their high chairs having breakfast. I asked Sunny if she had slept well.

"Oh, I was so afraid because everyone said the comrades were coming last night. But then I heard the singing, so I wasn't afraid any more."

"Sunny, you could not have heard the music. It was up by my house."

"I don't care what you heard," she said. "I heard the music outside my bedroom."

"In what language were the songs being sung?" I asked.

"I don't know," said Sunny.

"But you know five African languages."

She replied, "All I know is, something was special about that language."

"Well, the Lord sent it to encourage us, don't you think?"

She nodded her head. "Yes, that's what it was."

I went to check on a student whose husband was away on business and who had a young, ill daughter.

"How did you get on last night? Were you afraid without your husband?" I asked.

"Yes, I was terrified. But then I heard the singing."

"I heard it too! What language did they sing in?" I asked.

"Now that's a funny thing. I know quite a few languages, but there was something very different about that language."

"Well, the Lord really gave us something special to encourage us, didn't He?"

And she agreed.

When I got home, my two helpers had felt safe enough to return to work. As I was making breakfast and fixing tea, I told the ladies about the music I heard during the night. They both began jumping up and down and crying and clapping their hands.

"What's the matter?" I said.

"Oh, the Lord has protected you!"

"I know that. But who did the singing?"

Esther, my wonderful driver and helper, said "Give me your Bible."

I reached across the table and put the *Shangaan* Bible in her hands.

"Oh no, no, no. It must be the Bible in your mother tongue."

I went into my bedroom and got my English Bible. She opened it to Psalm 91 and read, "He shall give His angels charge over you" (v. 11 NKJV).

She glared at me. "Don't you believe what the Bible says?"

"Yes, of course I do. But who was singing?"

She put her hands on her hips and gave me a look that mothers give silly children. "You *heard* the angels this time, that's all."

I had no other answer. That music rang in my heart for a week. I don't remember it anymore, but I feel that one day I will be singing that praise song with all the African Christians in heaven.

The Journey
No One Chooses

KAT CRAWFORD

I screamed.

My husband lying in the bed next to me didn't move. I screamed louder.

Gary still didn't move, and neither did our border collie on the floor. The walnut paneling and thick drapes kept our bedroom dark even during daylight hours, so during the middle of the night in the utter blackness I could see nothing. Yet I could not move.

What kept me pinned to the bed?

I wanted to pray, to talk to the Lord, but the words didn't come. Screams ripped from deep inside. Was I losing my mind? Could it be a spirit of darkness—an evil spirit?

If I questioned my preacher husband, would he laugh at

me? He'd found signs of sacrificial idol worship north of town. He'd reported the burned carcass to the police, who said it was just kids delving in childish witchcraft—the badger, candles, and fire pit were harmless, the officers said.

Was it possible some sort of spirit from the site attached itself to Gary? Could he bring such a thing home? The whole scene felt like something from some movie, not like what happened in a parsonage bedroom.

Trembling, I slid my left arm to the edge of the bed, grabbed tight, rolled to the left, and slid from under the weight that held me down. My heart thumped loudly in our silent house while I stumbled to a rocker in our living room. A streetlamp sent slivers of light through the mini-blinds, lighting my way.

"Jesus! Jesus! Jesus!" I cried out when I slumped into the chair.

Instantly the sense of doom and darkness fled, but the fear of telling anyone or trying to describe the horrific event lingered.

Night after night the same scene occurred. During the day I could pretend things were normal—although I was tired, life went on as usual. My serene face masked my fears while I worked in the church office, visited nursing homes and shut-ins with Gary, and made the usual hospital visits.

I prayed constantly for God to protect our home and then wrote out Ephesians 6:16 and 18 to carry in my pocket and tape to the bathroom mirror.

> In addition to all this, take up your shield of faith, with which you can extinguish all the flaming arrows of the evil one. . . . And pray in the Spirit on all occasions with all kinds of prayers and requests. With this in mind, be alert and always keep on praying for all the Lord's people.

While Gary studied, I called on women and helped plan a Mother's Day Tea—I created special bulletins and sent letters to church members. I kept busy, busy, busy, doing anything to keep me from thinking about the nighttime ordeals.

Before bed I read my Bible and studied how evil spirits existed in Jesus' day. I knew they were real in the present world too. But fear kept me from telling Gary. I kept thinking that if I told him about the continual attacks, he'd think I exaggerated the experience.

My bedtime became later and later. Worn out, I'd fall asleep. Somewhere between that exhausted sleep and morning I would awaken in fear, my body trembling and pinned to the bed once more.

One night while sitting in my rocker, I cried out to Jesus. The evil darkness instantly disappeared. Tears of relief blinded my vision for a moment. Then I saw a boy and a girl, maybe eight and ten years old, dressed in the brightest white garments, walking toward me. They didn't frighten me, they simply appeared, their hands clasped. Before I could say or do anything, they disappeared.

For a few seconds I sat in peace. The children said nothing, but it seemed they encouraged me to tell Gary what happened.

I hurried to the bedroom.

"Hon, help me," I shook Gary awake. "A demon is attacking me." Gary didn't question anything I said. Although I'd lived through weeks of trauma, I detailed the turmoil in a few minutes.

Gary held me. Comforted me. Listened to me.

"Why didn't you tell me before?" he asked. When I began to cry he said, "Shh, it's all right now. It's all right."

Then he prayed. I don't remember everything he said, but he finished by saying, "Lord, we come before you in the name of Jesus. Place a shield around my wife. In Jesus' name. Amen."

I slept in peace and quiet wrapped in Gary's arms that night and the following nights.

A week later Gary said, "I totally understand your experience. Whatever this is . . . it's in our bedroom at night. I've battled. I've called out to you and the dog and neither of you move."

We held hands and prayed for God's protection.

A few weeks later we attended our denomination's annual meeting for the leaders in our part of the country. When it was time for Gary to give his report, he read off the usual statistics, finished with the necessary information for yearly reporting, and then raised his eyes to the hundreds that filled the sanctuary—pastors, their wives, and many laity. He stood silent a few moments, and then turned to address the leaders of our denomination on the platform.

Gary told of my battle with a spirit of darkness. He explained how he'd prayed with me and it left me alone—but then the spirit had attacked him.

"Depression has been dogging my heels for months now. I'm tired of fighting. I wish I had the courage to take my life," Gary said.

A pregnant silence filled the air when Gary walked down the aisle to sit by me. I grabbed his hand and watched helplessly while tears ran down his cheeks. I could hear many around us weeping—blowing their noses.

The leader called the next pastor to give his report as if Gary had said nothing unusual.

"Didn't you hear my husband?" I wanted to scream.

Out of the corner of my eye I saw someone on the far side of the room walk to the platform. He spoke to another leader.

When the current reporting pastor left the microphone, the other leader said, "Gary, will you please come to the altar. Men of God, come. Let's surround this man in prayer."

After the meeting finished, three pastors approached us.

"Don't ignore this spiritual warfare. It's real." One of them suggested we read books on spiritual warfare written by Neil Anderson. Another said, "As soon as you return home, find the strongest spiritual people of your church. Have them pray and anoint every window and door in your house and your church with oil."

We were armed with knowledge and covered in prayer, but how could we talk to our congregation about what had happened? Would they believe us?

The day after we arrived home, Gary called several members of our congregation together. He told them about our experiences and asked for their help.

We bathed our house and church in healing oil and prayer. The spirit fled.

Where did the spirit come from and why did we experience such nights of darkness?

Maybe we'll never know the full story, but soon after the "healing prayer," we learned that a high school student committed suicide after being involved with a group of teens delving in witchcraft. His mother formed a group of parents to bring light to the community. We knew from experience that what she talked about was real and harmful, and she and the teens needed our prayers. We met with the mother, told her about our experience, and assured her of our prayer support.

Those involved in the prayer over our home and church had their eyes opened in new understanding of the spirit world. The group continued to meet together to pray for our community and the youth involved in the demonic world.

One huge lesson I learned was that being a pastor's wife with biblical knowledge didn't keep me from fear of the darkness or embarrassment over talking to my husband about my experiences. I learned how important it is to share every problem—the enemy wanted me to keep my fears a secret.

The experience taught us about the needs of pastors. Gary's statement, "Depression has been dogging my heels. . . . I wish I had the courage to take my life," shocked those at the assembly, but many pastors and wives confessed their own weariness and sought help. Pastors wrote to us to thank Gary for his honesty. Other pastors had their eyes opened to the needs of parsonage families near them. Men of God began to meet together and lift each other in prayer.

We don't choose the journey, but God is always there and often uses the scariest events to touch our lives. In the process, He uses our experiences to reach others.

Voice of a Liar

JESSICA TALBOT

I never personally felt any touch of God's supernatural power until the day I stepped off a curb in downtown Vancouver right into the path of an oncoming bus.

That final step into death's path was actually a culmination of events that had begun a month earlier and eight thousand miles away in Australia.

My husband, Kyle, and I had left Canada four years before on our thirty-six-foot sailboat and traveled through the South Pacific, to New Zealand, and then to Australia. But there our sailing adventures abruptly halted.

Shortly after 11:00 p.m. on a March night, our yacht was rolled over by a freak wave during a storm in the Bass Strait, south of Australia. In seconds, Kyle was immobilized with head, rib, kidney, and back injuries, and the boat suffered major damage.

Standing amid the mess in the cabin, fully aware we were in danger of sinking any moment with a broken mast now poised to act as a battering ram, I felt an eerie void surround me and an inner voice whispered, *You're on your own now. God's not here. He doesn't care about you.*

In shock from the rollover, I never considered that these faith-battering thoughts were the work of a spiritual enemy.

Before the wave struck, I had been praying for twenty exhausting hours that God would save us from the storm.

Why keep praying? Just get busy! said the relentless voice.

With that, I turned my full attention to Kyle, who was on the floor of the cabin in severe pain, and relinquished any hope of divine intervention.

The next morning, Kyle could barely crawl to our ham radio.

"We have to get help," he whispered. Every word was a great effort for him. Working at a snail's pace while the storm roared unabated, we strung an antenna inside the yacht.

"Mayday, Mayday, Mayday," Kyle finally gasped into the microphone. To our relief, another radio operator responded immediately, and within two hours a dangerous air-sea rescue was underway to get us to land and to airlift Kyle to the hospital.

After he was released from the hospital, we returned to Sydney with the help of friends, and only then did I remember my visitor's visa would expire in a few days.

When I explained our predicament to Immigration, the unsympathetic tone of the officer stunned me.

"You'll have to leave the country to renew your visa," he said. "Your husband can stay because he's injured, but you must go."

Two days later, I was on an airplane back to Vancouver, leaving Kyle behind on our disabled yacht.

At Vancouver airport, I waved enthusiastically to my mother and sister, who were standing in the crowd waiting to greet me. We hugged each other and started toward the car for the drive home. My parents were both in precarious health and had moved in with my sister and her family shortly after Kyle and I left Canada.

"I want to tell you something," my sister said, drawing me aside. "A man phoned from Australia and said he heard on the radio that you were missing at sea in a storm and likely dead. With her bad heart, that would have killed Mom if she'd answered the phone. I never told her about the call. And I didn't believe it was true."

"How can that be?" I asked. "No one knew anything about us until we sent out the Mayday call! So how could the media have reported us missing?"

"I don't know," she replied. "He said he just wanted to let us know."

I remembered the eerie void I had experienced right after the rollover and felt that same sensation wash over me again. *Why would someone tell my family we were probably dead?*

For the first time since the accident, I began to wonder if some spiritual force wanted to harm us.

During the drive to my sister's home, I finally began to relax and remarked, "It sure feels strange to be driving on the right side of the road again after all this time. I'll have to be careful in traffic until I get used to it!"

Once I was settled in with my family, I applied for a visa to return to Australia. A letter arrived about ten days later and I opened it excitedly. I missed Kyle and was eager to return.

As I quickly scanned the letter, my mind went numb. My application was denied. The letter said that I would have to wait at least a year before a new visa could be considered.

I phoned Kyle and wailed. "It's crazy. I told them you and the boat are still in Australia! But they won't let me back in. What will we do?"

With that, I started to cry.

"Try not to worry," Kyle consoled. "I'll get a lawyer and work on it from this end."

As we hung up I wanted to pray, but the same inner voice that visited me the night of the rollover said, *God won't hear you, so don't look to Him for help!*

I believed the voice.

Not wanting to mope around my sister's house, I decided to take a trip into downtown Vancouver to see what had changed while we were gone.

"It's very different," said my sister. "They built a pedestrian mall and now only buses and taxis are allowed on the street in that area."

A bit of sight-seeing sounded like exactly what I needed to lift my mood. I traveled an hour on the bus to reach downtown, but the trip was well worth it.

"It's beautiful," I said to a nearby stranger as I drank in the view. She smiled and nodded but moved quickly away.

The hours passed quickly.

There's just time for a coffee before I must head back, I thought as I looked at my watch. Directly across the street was a coffee shop, so after checking carefully for oncoming traffic, I stepped off the curb.

I was beyond the point of no return when I saw an enormous bus bearing rapidly down on me!

In a flash I realized I had looked the wrong way for oncoming traffic and was about to die for that mistake. With the bus only feet away, I had no time to pray.

Suddenly, a ferociously strong wind struck the front of me and I felt invisible hands on my shoulders lifting and pushing me back up on the curb, setting me on the sidewalk until I regained my balance and the bus was safely past.

The wind stopped instantly. I looked around.

No one appeared to notice. . . . The leaves on the trees were still and there was no hint that any breeze had blown. Not a hair on any pedestrian was ruffled.

I began to shake. I knew God had sent an angel to preserve my life. I couldn't stop trembling as I realized how close I had come to death and that I would have died angry with God.

Spiritual light flooded into my soul. I understood that the voice that had been turning me away from God and attacking my prayers ever since the night of the accident was a demonic enemy of my soul. It came at a vulnerable time and spoke lies into my mind. Not only was this spirit attacking me, but it wanted to harm my family as well.

My being surged with an uncontrollable burst of gratitude to God. I thanked Him over and over again for life . . . for *saving* me, for saving Kyle, for sparing my family!

God *had* heard my every prayer, but I'd been unable to believe this because of the damage and injuries and the distance I allowed between myself and God.

As I reviewed the details of our rescue and subsequent events, I saw clearly the loving care provided by God. From that moment, the evil whisperings ceased. The enemy lost his power over my mind and I felt a loving Father gather me back to Him with forgiveness.

While I rejoiced with God on the streets of Vancouver, Kyle was successfully arranging a visa for me so I could soon return to Australia. In my heart, I knew God was fully in charge of that process as well, and that He would be right there with us when Kyle and I could at last celebrate our reunion.

Thank You for Not Smoking

LIZ COLLARD

There was no question: I was an addict.

I had smoked for more than thirty-five years. Every morning, the first thing I did was smoke a cigarette. Every night, the last thing I did was smoke a cigarette. In between, I smoked after I ate, while talking on the phone, when I got in the car, before I walked into wherever I was going—at almost every point of every day of my life.

My father was a smoker when I was growing up, and my two sisters and I experimented with smoking in our teen years. I've often wondered why I was the only one who immediately got hooked.

Toni's brief association with tobacco products was almost comical. We always knew when she had been smoking because she came home with a greenish cast to her face and spent the rest of the evening in the upstairs bathroom. Before long she gave up trying.

Wendi handled smoking like everything else she did. She mastered it but did not let it master her. She was a social smoker and had little trouble quitting when she decided to do so.

I was not so lucky.

I have never tried meth or been a coke addict, but I've read about how quickly a person can become addicted to them. That was my experience with cigarettes. Once I started at age thirteen, I could not turn back.

I married a man who was also a smoker. By then, the habit was such an ingrained part of my life, I never thought about it much. I didn't see it as a problem until our first child was born. At that point, three things began to change my feelings about smoking.

Our son Matthew was born in the early 1980s when bans on smoking in public places were becoming widespread. Public opinion was shifting and, over the next few years, we would see a decidedly anti-smoking feeling permeate our society. I'm not sure when I noticed that people were beginning to look down on smokers, but I felt it more keenly as time went by. I became more and more secretive about my habit.

Around that time, we started hearing about the health risks associated with secondhand smoke. My husband and I decided to quit smoking in the house. We live in Florida, so I was spared the torture of snatching a few drags while shivering in below-freezing weather—except while visiting relatives up north. But I could no longer light up whenever and wherever I wanted. Smoking was becoming a hassle, and I was starting to wish I could give it up.

The third factor was that when Matthew was a toddler, I rededicated my life to Christ. I had accepted Jesus as my Savior when I was in elementary school but fell away from Him during my teen years. Becoming a wife and mother motivated me to renew my relationship with God.

I started going to church, and thankfully my husband soon followed. He became a Christian and we were baptized together. We got involved in a home group and Bible study. I joined the choir and became active in the women's ministry.

But I didn't quit smoking. I didn't even try to cut down. The only difference was now I felt guilty about it. I had this secret sin I needed to hide from everyone. I would still puff away in the car before we pulled into the church parking lot, but I was careful to blow it out the window so I wouldn't smell like smoke when I got inside.

For the next twenty years, I wrestled with my addiction. I knew the reasons I should quit and understood the dangers to my children and me.

In spite of that, I smoked all the way through my next two pregnancies. We still went outside to smoke at home, but I continued to do it in the car. Though I didn't want to admit it, my kids were often exposed to secondhand smoke.

As for myself, I rationalized that my father had smoked for many more years than I had, and he was fine. And he smoked *unfiltered* cigarettes. Sadly, my dad died from heart problems when he was only sixty-three years old.

I could justify the health risks, but the spiritual implications of my addiction became increasingly bothersome. I was ashamed to be a smoker and felt like a hypocrite for calling myself a Christian while I continued my pack-a-day habit. As I grew in spiritual maturity, I couldn't deny that it was a stronghold in my life.

My need to smoke controlled me. I planned my life around it. I always had to make sure I had enough cigarettes on hand. If I felt like I didn't, I panicked. I often drove to the store late at night so I would have them in the morning when I woke up. I couldn't commit to any event that lasted longer than a few hours if I couldn't smoke there. Overnight trips—like a mission trip or retreat—were out of the question.

I suspected my smoking hindered my relationship with Christ in many ways. If I could only get free from the bondage of the cigarettes, I sensed it would open a whole new realm for me.

There was one big problem: I didn't want to quit. I enjoyed smoking, and in spite of all the reasons I knew I should give it up, I had no intention of actually doing so.

I occasionally prayed, "Lord, give me the desire to quit!" But for the most part I just kept on smoking.

By this time, my husband and I were lay leaders of the marriage ministry at our church. Every Tuesday night for more than four years, we stood in front of hundreds of couples and encouraged them to trust God for all they needed in their marriages and in their lives. We then walked out and lit up as we headed home.

In the fall of 2009, I was working on writing the third and final part of a curriculum for the marriage ministry, and I was on a spiritual mountaintop. It seemed like God was revealing new truths to me every day, and I felt invincible—like nothing could pull me away from the amazing fellowship I was enjoying moment by moment with Him.

The lessons I had been working on for the curriculum opened my eyes to many things about who we are in Christ. A new understanding was dawning regarding what we have available to us as children of the King and co-heirs with

His Son. My prayers were energized as never before, and for several days I had been praying for two or more hours every morning.

After my family left for work and school on November 5, I carried my Bible, prayer book, and cigarettes to the bench in our backyard where I always sat. Automatically, my hands reached for the pack and lighter, and I lit my first cigarette of the morning. I inhaled, held it for a few seconds, and then blew it out, enjoying the tiny buzz I felt as the nicotine entered my system.

I was raising the cigarette to take another drag when it hit me.

If I really believe God can do anything, why am I still smoking?

With my next thought, I casually tossed off a prayer: *God, deliver me from smoking.*

It was so offhand, I didn't even pause from what I was doing. I placed the cigarette in my mouth and inhaled again.

But this time, when I went to blow it out, something strange happened. Instead of a solid white stream of smoke, I was shocked to see what looked like semi-transparent, puffy black clouds coming out of my mouth. They slowly floated up and away, even when I tried to blow harder.

I thought I must have imagined it. So I took another drag of the cigarette. I tried to blow out the smoke, but the same thing happened.

I still couldn't believe I was actually seeing this. To make sure, I deliberately inhaled a third time. Once again, the black clouds came floating out of my mouth. I bent over and put out the cigarette in the grass at my feet.

It was the last one I ever smoked.

My desire to smoke was gone. I did not experience any physical withdrawal or struggle in any way to overcome the addiction.

Over the next few days and weeks, there were times when I was tempted. But I would say to myself, *God has delivered me from smoking. I am free from the bondage I was in and I will not return to it,* and the urge quickly passed. Those moments came less and less often, and soon I didn't have them at all.

Praise God, I was free.

Most people would agree that kind of instant deliverance from a thirty-five-year addiction is a miracle, but it's not the end of the story.

A little more than two weeks after my experience in the backyard, my whole world came crashing down. Problems had been in our lives, but I hadn't really paid attention to them. Now I was forced to. All at once, I found myself financially devastated, my husband was hospitalized, our ministry was shut down, and many of our friends turned away from us. Almost everything that gave me a sense of security or comfort was suddenly ripped from my life.

But with all the stress I felt, I didn't start smoking again.

More important, throughout that time of devastation, when I often had no idea where we would get our next meal or how I would live through the rest of the day, I did not despair.

I had nowhere to turn except to God. But He had delivered me from smoking. And I knew He did it to give me the strength, the faith, and the unwavering trust I needed to make it through all that was to follow. I kept thinking, *He delivered me from this; He will surely take care of us.*

And He did.

A while back I celebrated the one-year anniversary of the day I was freed from the bondage of smoking. Since then,

I have seen God do many more miracles. He has provided for us and worked things out in ways I could never have anticipated.

And I can say with total assurance, "The Lord is my rock, my fortress and my deliverer" (Psalm 18:2).

When Time Stood Still

CRAIG CORNELIUS, as told to BILLY BURCH

The last place I wanted to be was in a hospital room. All hospital rooms seem the same—off-white walls, plastic trim, stainless handles, the smell of disinfectant, and the sense of uncertainty.

But I was there because the ambulance brought me and I couldn't get around that. I was getting the attention any patient would have wanted, but I really didn't need to be there.

Okay, so I passed out earlier in the day. No big deal. I had been under a lot of stress recently, so a few seconds of unconsciousness due to a nervous breakdown or whatever was no surprise. One can't hide stress or stuff it down too long before it shows itself. That much I knew.

I lay on the hospital bed, my upper body tilted to forty-five degrees. My wife and kids stood around me as the doctors debated whether I was cleared to leave or not. All the test results indicated that I could go. I would have been out of there if it weren't for one doctor who strongly advised I stay for further testing. But I had a hunting trip lined up that night and needed to leave. Soon.

After finishing dinner, I pushed the tray aside. A numbing sensation slowly crept up my head. I glanced at my boys, reached for them, and asked my wife to get the nurse.

Suddenly, my eyes rolled back as I dropped onto my pillow. The monitor flat-lined. My heart stopped. I lost all connection to this world.

My journey into the world of death had actually begun one night a few months earlier. I remember I was sitting behind a computer wearing jeans and a maroon shirt, clothes I'd worked in that day.

At that moment, I had one objective: find a new motor for my boat. I had just hung up the phone from talking to my mom and dad, wishing them a great time while they were on a trip, and wishing Mom a happy seventieth birthday.

The phone rang again twenty minutes later. My wife, Debbie, answered it, and I could tell it was Mom again.

"Hey, Mom. Having a good time? Everything okay?"

Debbie smiled at me, but then her smile turned to shock.

"What?" gasped Debbie. "What hospital are they taking him to?"

Holding her hand over the phone, Debbie looked right at me. "Craig, your dad just had a heart attack!" We packed our bags and drove as quickly as we could to Anne Arundel County, Maryland.

A nurse greeted us at the hospital. Nobody had to say anything. I saw Mom down the hallway.

"They tried, but Dad didn't make it," Mom said softly.

No, this couldn't be real. My dad, my hunting partner of thirty-two years, the one and only Dad.

Someone tell me it's a bad dream. Please.

As He has done for so many, God sent numbness. Divine Novocain. A soothing ointment to soften the blow. Whatever you want to call it, it got me through the funeral and even a few weeks after. But as with all painkillers, the numbness faded with time, giving way to something much heavier: grief, depression, and unanswered questions.

No one rebounds quickly from such a devastating event. My thoughts sank into a thick fog, and I was losing my bearings. My emotional tank was empty, and there I stalled, floating in the dark waters of unanswered questions.

Why now? I would scream to myself.

Where is God in all this? I would beg to know. *Does He hear me or my prayers?*

Is there even a heaven? And can I be sure Dad is there? My thoughts confused me.

You see, I grew up a Christian and knew all the answers. Dad and the church taught me well. I should have known without a doubt that Dad was with God. But doubt drifted in, and I drifted out and didn't know how to get back.

Eventually, I returned to work. People told me it would be good to move on. I wasn't so sure, but couldn't come up with anything better. I also made plans to head back out later that week with some hunting buddies. Though it would be hard without Dad, I knew it would bring some healing I desperately needed. I just had to get through one more day of work, and then leave for the cabin that evening.

That morning was like any other. I felt great. I was looking

121

forward to getting the workday behind me, heading down the road, and meeting the guys at the cabin.

At work, I was scheduled to preview a job site with my boss, John. I normally handled that on my own. But John had all the notes and knew all the details, so I nearly fought with him just to go. He finally gave in.

Upon arriving at the job site, I began measuring the walls. But the room seemed to spin below my feet. John drove me back to the shop. I entered the showroom, tried to sit on the couch, and then hit the floor face-first.

"Someone call 9-1-1!" John yelled as he rushed to my side.

Minutes later the EMTs arrived.

"Looks like you're coming with us," they said.

My wife tried to contact our family doctor to see if I could get an appointment at his office instead of going to the ER, but there were no openings. So I was on my way.

At the hospital, they ran a series of tests. The ER doctors came to discuss the results.

"We don't have a clear idea what happened," said one. "We have a couple more tests we want to run. One is an ultrasound check on your carotid artery. That could tell us something. We also want to run a Lyme disease test and a few others."

"Why can't my doctor run these tests at another time?" I protested. "I really need to be somewhere tonight."

"Well," they answered. "You could go. But it will take months before you get the appointments and a whole lot more in co-pays. We can take care of all the tests within the next twenty-four hours if we admit you for the night."

I was still prepared to check out when my father-in-law spotted one of his neighbors, who was the head of the emergency room. Some of my family members asked him for his opinion.

"Here is where it stands," he said. "Though the test results show us no red flags, things have escalated in the prognosis as a result of Craig's family history and the recent death of his father. Hearing all of the circumstances, I think it would be in Craig's best interest to admit him overnight for further testing."

We questioned his judgment, but he insisted. Again, I had no control in this situation. It was three o'clock in the afternoon when they admitted me for an overnight stay.

My wife brought my three sons from school. Entering the room, they looked at me with eyes of uncertainty. It's hard for any kid to see his dad lying on a hospital bed.

"I'll be fine," I said. "You don't have to worry about a thing."

"Are you going hunting?" asked my oldest.

"No, that's out," I said. "They need to run more tests overnight. So you guys want to stay with me here to watch the Eagles game?"

They nodded as I ate my mac and cheese. Finishing my meal, I began pushing the tray away from me.

"Hey, Deb," I said. "I'm not feeling so great. Can you get the nurse?"

When Deb and the nurse returned, they found me lying on my bed with my fists clenched and my eyes rolled back. The monitor made a continuous beeping sound, setting an alarm off at the nurses' station.

"Craig! Craig!" screamed Debbie as she slapped my face. "Craig! Wake up!"

Three more nurses burst into the room. Debbie hustled our boys out.

The doctor and a nurse reviewed the strip. My heart had completely stopped. The three electrical systems in my heart failed, so the defibrillator would be useless.

I was not prepared for the life-changing moment that was about to happen. When my heart stopped, time seemed to stop as well. I sensed a feeling that I can only liken to being pulled out of a wet suit. I felt myself slowly moving forward.

I felt a tremendous sense of peace and well-being. The scenery was in high definition, crisp and sharp. Everything around me had an amazing iridescence to it. The colors shone like those that emerged when my kids used to blow bubbles in the direct sunlight—only much more intense and on a larger scale.

I noticed a figure standing a short distance away. I quickly saw that it was my father. His hair was parted as it always was, but was darker in color as it had been when he was younger. I also noticed as I approached him that he wasn't wearing his glasses—though he'd worn them for as long as I can recall. I clearly remember his arms reaching toward me as if to gently push me back or stop my forward progress.

"Not now. Not right now," he said. Then he disappeared.

As quickly as I came, I started to leave. I sensed the feeling of fighting my way out of a bag, similar to that "wet suit" feeling. As I began to regain my bearings, I noticed many people around me, including several nurses and doctors on both sides of my bed. As my vision focused, my mind cleared. I saw Debbie standing next to me.

"I saw my dad! I felt like I was fighting my way out of a bag!" I told her.

The doctors, having quickly diagnosed the problem with my heart, rushed me down the hall to insert a temporary pacemaker. The whole episode lasted only thirty seconds according to the printout on the electrocardiogram, but it felt like an eternity.

Few events in anyone's life make time stand still. This was one for me. It's funny sometimes how God answers our questions. All of mine were answered in that short time. I don't know why God chose to answer me in that way, but I am better because of it.

Is God in control? Yes. Does He hear my prayers? Yes. Is heaven real? Definitely. Do I trust God more now? You bet.

And now I know that I have a purpose greater than I ever thought. "Not now" means there is more for me to do and more for me to know about God's love. I can't help but think that my newfound purpose might be a combination of spreading the reality of His love through His Son and sharing the reality of a life beyond this one.

I guess heart failure is what it took to bring my faith to where it is now. I am the proud owner of a permanent pacemaker and a renewed faith in my Maker.

Hear No Evil

LAURA CHEVALIER

And these bullets landed here in this bed while Samson and Gladys were in it!"

My neighbor, a Kenyan momma named Mercy, looked at me and fingered the projectiles in her hand. She was filling me in on what had happened in the small rustic guesthouse that served as a stopping-off point for many missionaries and other travelers who came through the dusty, remote Kenyan town. There were two apartments on the floor below the guesthouse, and I rented the one beneath the room we were standing in.

Incredibly, the bullets Mercy held had not harmed the occupants of the bed. But what was even more incredible to me was that I, typically a light sleeper, had slept soundly through the night while an evil man attacked our building at point-blank range with an AK-47.

The room where we now stood was the last one the bullets had passed through. First, they had shattered the front window. Then they had bounced off the kitchen counter and raced through the walls of the bathroom and an adjacent guestroom as if those walls were made of paper.

Finally, the bullets passed through this last guestroom wall and landed in the disheveled bed now in front of me.

As we retraced our steps, Mercy pointed out where sleeping guests would have been hit if they had been present. Thankfully the other rooms had been empty.

Earlier that morning I'd noticed people gathering outside. Because this was rather unusual, I had joined them to find out what was happening. The white-haired missionary who lived in the apartment next to mine stared at me and asked me how I had fared through the night. I just looked at her, confused.

"You mean you slept through it?" she'd exclaimed.

My shocked neighbors gathered around to recount the facts from the previous night. Everyone had spent the night sleeplessly huddled in corners.

Everyone except me.

The other missionary said she'd crawled down to the end of her hall, whispering loudly through the wall and tapping on it to see if I was all right, but I never heard her even though our walls were so thin.

As they continued to talk about the night, immediately I saw a picture in my mind of large hands covering my ears— hands so large that they seemed to engulf my head from above. They were gently holding my head, shielding me from the noise.

I realized at that moment that someone—an angel or Jesus himself—had stood above me and held my ears and head throughout the attack. I could see evidence of the attack, but I had no memory of it. As a result, the loud noises that startled my neighbors did not startle me in the days that followed.

The next few days and weeks were really hard. Those investigating discovered that this attack on our building was actually the second one. They found more bullet holes around my fellow missionary's back windows.

When this was brought to our attention, we realized that we'd all heard the gunfire on an earlier night, but because the shooter had been much farther away, no one realized it was directed at our compound.

Due to these scare tactics, those in authority over my missionary friend thought it was unsafe for her to remain, so my friend left the country.

Though there were rumors of who might have been behind the attack, the police did not discover the shooter. He remained unchecked.

The fact that no one was ever convicted of the crime bothered me. I was also frustrated by my friend's departure. I struggled with questions like, *Why me, God? Why this? What possible good can you bring out of this situation? How long do I have to bear with this uncertainty?*

He answered me with His own set of questions: *Do you trust me? Are you willing to learn and grow? Are you going to rebel at every hint of hardship, or are you going to let me carry you through? Are you willing to follow me whatever the cost?*

I'd like to say that God's questions immediately caused me to react better to my circumstances. In many ways they did. I served in my role whole-heartedly, but beneath the surface I harbored some anger and frustration. I wanted things to be resolved, for deeds done in darkness to be brought into the light. When days passed and that did not happen, I became resentful.

Nearly two years later, while I was enjoying a spiritual retreat, God whispered to me with a startling question from the book of Jonah that I was studying. He asked, "Why are you so angry?"

The question was so sharp, but at first I thought, *Well, am I really angry? What am I angry about?*

Floods of images flashed in front of me, a silent movie bringing conviction. But I wanted to argue with God; I felt my anger was righteous. All I wanted was justice.

God began revealing to me how I had let resentment and bitterness grow. It was time to let go and forgive, and let Him handle the justice. And I am happy to report that I did.

God's patience with me is humbling. As I look back and wonder why God chose to protect me in that way that night in Kenya, I can see His sovereign hands at work.

I stayed in that community for another year. Would I have stayed if I had witnessed the attack? I don't know. What I do know is that I did not fear or fret.

Some might say I should have feared—the danger was real. But I cannot remember dwelling on the violence of the attack or being anxious about another one. I wasn't scared of someone coming after me. That kind of fear was completely absent.

Though I missed my friend and wished things had worked out differently, God provided many new friends—Kenyans and Koreans. Her absence also created the space for me to mature and serve in ways that I would not have if she had remained.

So what man meant for harm, God meant for good. His protection and grace during that time reassures me that wherever I go, He is sovereign over my plans. He continues to hold me gently but firmly in the palm of His hands, and because of that I rest easy.

The Well-Dressed Devil

BEATRICE FISHBACK

After six years, my marriage was on the rocks. Although not physically separated, my husband, Jim, and I were emotionally separated and no longer enjoyed each other's company.

Jim had begged me to go to church with him in a last-ditch effort to save our relationship.

"No," I said. After all, why would I attend church with someone who didn't show love to me at home?

Selfishness somehow has a way of making our attitudes seem justified and sanctimonious. So I felt a certain sense of superiority and pride thinking I had hurt Jim in the process of denying a very important element in our marriage—God.

I blamed Jim for our marital problems, but actually I was self-centered and self-absorbed. I wanted things to go my way whenever a decision was made—big or small. So we fought over everything. And I always had to be right.

He eventually stopped speaking to me and communication became impossible.

My stubborn actions toward Jim also hardened my love toward God. I no longer wanted to attend church and finally convinced myself that God no longer existed. So my marriage drifted and my relationship with God became stunted.

God does not necessarily take us where we think we want to go. And there are times He takes drastic measures to get our attention and keep us from making huge errors. That's exactly what He did with me—and in living, dreaming color.

It was another night of silent stubbornness. Jim's stiff back facing me attested to the fact that once again we had gone to bed with no communication between us. Obstinately I slung around and turned my back to his and fell into a deep sleep.

I dreamed I was on a ship—a beautiful cruise ship with a long promenade and glittering lights. It was a star-studded evening and the moon beamed with supernatural radiance.

I was wearing a long evening dress that caressed my chest and hips in sultry elegance. My shoulders were slung back with confidence and self-assurance as I strolled alone along the deck and gazed at the stars. The entire setting was as glorious as the heavenly sky.

I noticed someone coming toward me. A man. Somehow I knew that I didn't want to speak to anyone, especially to a man. So I turned away and gazed upward, this time holding on to the ship's railing. Yet each time I turned, the well-dressed man was closer than the time before.

Finally, he stood right beside me. He was dressed in a black tuxedo, his pant legs pressed with starched precision. The cummerbund around his waist peeked out from under a tailored jacket. The buttons on his white shirt glittered like jewels.

He was tall, dark, and handsome. His chiseled chin and smooth dark hair complemented his warm smile and complexion. He was every woman's dream of the perfect man—attractive, debonair, and charming.

I looked up into his eyes. He gazed at me with self-possession.

"What do you want from me? Why are you following me?" I asked.

He smiled and spoke softly, yet his words were not gentle or enticing. In fact, they seemed to grab me by the throat and squeeze. My heart thumped and eerie goose bumps shivered up my arms.

"I am the devil, and I want your soul."

A well-dressed devil stood on my ship and offered me his world. Then he was gone. The ship, the beautiful evening, and my stunning dress—it all vanished.

I woke up in a sweat. The dream was as real as the bed I was sleeping in. I could clearly recall every sensation as if the situation had actually happened.

And I knew somehow it had.

Jim's back still faced me. The coverlet over us was a warm, familiar comfort to my mind and body. Yet I knew without a doubt that God had given me a glimpse into what my mind was dwelling on—leaving my husband and adopting the world—and what that would ultimately mean. The things of the world do come prettily dressed. They are as thrilling as a well-dressed man who offers seduction and perfection—at least temporarily.

God showed me very clearly in my dream that I could choose the things of the world or return to Him, the God of my youth. I had the freedom of choice, but He wanted me to see what that choice would mean: selling my soul to a well-dressed devil.

I woke Jim up at three in the morning and told him I wanted to go to church. In a dazed stupor, he nodded and went back to sleep.

A few weekends later I attended a women's retreat the church offered. Throughout the weekend I heard over and over again about God's love. My eyes were opened to my selfishness in my marriage and my spiritual pride. That Sunday morning I recommitted my life to God and rededicated my heart to Jim.

The night on the ship with the well-dressed devil saved my marriage. And my life was forever altered when God reached into the recesses of my dream and dragged me back to the reality of life.

And I am eternally grateful that He did.

Amy's Amazing Rescue

DONALD E. PHILLIPS

Amy seemed like a normal, respectful, conscientious student in the Midwestern Bible institute where I was an administrator, teacher, and pastor.

Amy was pleasant and friendly—but we didn't know her smiles masked deep, dark, disturbing problems. We later learned that before she'd begun attending the school, Amy had been hospitalized in a mental institution and had some encounters with occult activity.

Now, as a student, Amy lived in a college apartment. Before long, some neighboring students started reporting strange things happening in the apartments—especially Amy's. They started seeing kitchenware and other objects randomly rising and floating through the air.

When the reports first began circulating, none of us on

staff knew exactly what to do. I was concerned for the safety of the students who lived in the apartments. No one reported any injury, but the events were contrary to the Bible college's Christian beliefs. We believed in Jesus as the light of the world and opposed the darkness of any demonic or satanic activity.

So something needed to be done.

Two of my co-workers, Roger and Jared, and I decided to investigate. We made an appointment to visit Amy and, on that day, Amy met us at the door, welcoming us politely. Her roommate, who knew why we were there, went into another room, but Amy sat alone on a small sofa. Roger, Jared, and I sat on another sofa about six feet away.

At first we had a relaxed, normal conversation with Amy—a chat about how she was doing in the college and personally. Before we could transition from relaxed conversation to serious concerns about what had happened in her apartment, something suddenly happened to Amy.

Amy's eyes glazed over and then became wild. This young woman, who had sat erect and polite, began to roll off the sofa, writhing, turning, contorting herself, doubtless being twisted by a demonic force.

We stayed calm due to our faith in the power of Christ over all powers. But suddenly we had to dramatically shift from the realm of natural human behavior and communication to a realm of supernatural conflict. Ephesians 6:12 came to my mind: "For our struggle is not against flesh and blood, but against the rulers, against the authorities, against the powers of this dark world and against the spiritual forces of evil in the heavenly realms."

It seemed that conflict in the heavenly realms was demonstrating its power on earth. After all, how often do people roll off sofas in front of guests and begin to flail on the floor—especially when their guests are ministers and their teachers!

As anger darkened Amy's eyes, her rational mind that had been communicating with us seemed far away. She sneered, she hissed, she snarled, she spewed out hatefulness. She even foamed at the mouth. With contorted lips and a grimace, she began pouring out strange names and words; it all seemed related to demons and occult powers.

As she rolled about on the floor, we prayed for her and called upon the name of Jesus to deliver her.

But the force commanding her body was not releasing her. As we carefully and gently approached her, we extended hands to her as a point of contact for prayer. Roger, a very kind, comforting gentleman, made the mistake of getting a bit too close to Amy. Amy, or perhaps more accurately, the demon controlling her at that time, kicked Roger hard between the legs.

Finally Amy was stilled. Not by us, though we continued praying through the entire experience. We kept imploring God through the name and power of Jesus Christ to free her from these evil forces just as Jesus freed demon-possessed people during His earthly ministry.

What did we learn? We experienced firsthand what may be called an exorcism, an expelling of the demonic in a spiritually captive person. We also saw demonstration of the fact that Satan is mighty but God is *almighty*. The power of Jesus' name is greater than any name in heaven or earth. That name has power to cast out darkness and destruction.

The deliverance session occurred on a Saturday. The next day we were all back in the main church assembly, including Amy. She looked like a completely different person—liberated, peaceful, and smiling. Those who knew her well marveled at the difference and radiance in her appearance. Students and staff members shared smiles and hugs with her with the conviction that she was now dramatically changed.

After this amazing rescue, after being pulled out of a dark sea of evil, Amy was restored to her right and best mind, knowing the wholeness of Christ above all the forces of evil He conquered and is still conquering.

The Sweet Touch of a Small Hand

PATTI SHENE

O range flames licked the wooden structure of our home. Black smoke from the blaze spread over the snow, turning its glistening white surface to a dingy, lifeless gray.

Only moments before, my little brother, younger sister, and I had scurried through our routine of preparations for school. *Would we even have school?* We pressed our noses against the window, the desire to extend our Christmas vacation burning in our hearts. Thanks to deep snow and sub-zero temperatures, we might get our wish to stay home another day.

The three wood-burning stoves that heated our comfortable home represented warmth and security—until the moment I saw flames and smoke spewing from the confines of the chimney. When I screamed for Mom, she raced into the room. Snapping the telephone receiver from its cradle with one hand, she motioned my sister and me outside with the other. We watched through the door in horror as Mom dropped the telephone and disappeared into billows of black smoke.

Despite her desperation, the searing heat and thick, acrid cloud forced her back. Somewhere on that second floor my five-year-old brother waited, innocent and vulnerable.

Dad had been chopping wood outside when our shrieks of panic focused his attention on the flames that erupted through the roof. The bulky clothing that encased his body, necessary to protect his skin against the below-zero weather, gave him enough protection to charge into the ruthless inferno. Even from where I stood outside, shivering with cold and terror, Dad's deep voice echoed in my ears as he shouted Bobby's name.

An eternity passed before Dad appeared with my baby brother cradled in his arms. Blistered, charred skin replaced Bobby's once pink, soft cheeks. I watched in disbelief as Dad hurled my brother's blackened body into a snow bank. *Was he breathing?*

Fire sirens wailed above the crackle of the greedy flames. A fireman asked Mom what she wanted snatched from the relentless flames if anything could be saved. A few moments later, several men maneuvered our huge grand piano out the door and across the frozen ground to safety.

"Where's Bobby?" Mom wailed, her voice hoarse from the smoke that filled the entire yard. She frantically scoured the snowbanks for any sign of her wounded son.

"We moved him to one of the sheds where he'd be more protected," a man responded.

Our neighbor, the local grocer, placed Bobby in his vehicle, and Mom accompanied them to the hospital. Before they left, the words I heard provoked more of a chill than the frigid temperatures. "The boy's not going to make it. He's too badly hurt."

Someone grabbed my hand and led me away. Numb with cold and shock, I followed. Once inside the warmth of my neighbor's house, I took up a vigil at the front window. For hours I sat there, resisting all efforts to pry me from that dreadful scene of devastation next door. Stunned into paralyzed silence, I watched my house burn to the ground.

We spent our first night without a home of our own with my aunt, uncle, and cousins. The two girls were the same age as my sister and me, and the four of us had stuck together through good times and bad. Their attempts to comfort me failed miserably. Two of my family members lay in hospital beds, fighting for their lives.

Dad had escaped serious burns but struggled for every breath due to smoke inhalation. Bobby teetered between life and death. He could croak out a few words, but couldn't swallow even water. The hospital staff did all they could to ease my brother's excruciating pain, but burn centers that provided specialized care did not exist then.

After a fitful, restless night, I woke to the sound of my aunt gagging in the bathroom. *Was she sick?* No, I had seen her stomach reject its contents in the past when something was terribly wrong. Her pale face and the grief in her eyes told me quicker than words that my worst nightmare had come true.

My baby brother was dead.

School that next day passed in a blur of unreality. My teacher hugged me. My classmates stared at me. The kids spoke in low tones, and conversation suspiciously stopped when I drew near. One small whisper spilled into my ears. "We're not supposed to talk to her about it."

Everyone in our sparsely populated Wisconsin town attended Bobby's funeral. We'd lost everything, but neighbors came together and donated the material goods that met our needs. One man even loaned us his house. Kids brought toys and Christmas decorations since the holiday season was still in full swing.

The generosity and love of our small community failed to pierce my hardened heart. My brother's death had etched a gaping hole in my life. Nothing would ever fill it.

Life resumed its ebb and flow for my family. Dad returned to his job on the lakes as an oarsman. Classes at school continued as if nothing had happened. For me, though, normal ceased to exist. I wrapped myself in a cocoon of anger, resentment, and pain. My ten-year-old heart rejected all the promises I'd been raised to believe about God.

What kind of God would let Bobby die like that? I hurled the bitter words toward heaven in a torrent of hateful protest against God's injustice. I cried all the time. No explanation answered the question of why my brother had to leave us. Sunday school lessons fell on deaf ears and my faith left me empty inside.

Three months after my brother's death, as I lay in my bed, hot tears collected in my eyes and streamed down my cheeks onto my pillow. My anger at God seethed in my broken heart. *How could you be so mean to take Bobby away?* I raged once again. I clenched my fists and stared into the vacant darkness.

Suddenly, a bright glow bathed the room. Gentle as the brush of a bird's feather, a small hand curled into my palm. The soft, familiar fingers of my little brother intertwined with mine. Countless times in the past I had reached out to him, his small hand nestled in the protective grip of his older sister.

Immediately, I recognized his sweet touch.

"Why are you crying? I'm happy where I am." Bobby's words melted my embittered heart. "Everything is okay. Don't cry for me anymore."

Warmth settled on the top of my head and traveled the length of my body until it reached clear down to my toes.

I bolted straight up in my bed. Had my sister reached over and taken my hand? I glanced to her side of the room. No. Her back faced me and her even breath indicated that she was asleep.

God does care about me!

I carried that truth with me as I nestled under the covers and fell into the most peaceful sleep I had experienced since that terrible day of the fire.

The next morning, I crept downstairs and greeted Mom in the kitchen. "Mom, Bobby held my hand last night and told me he is okay."

Would she believe me?

Mom blinked, and a smile spread across her face.

"Sit," she urged. We settled ourselves at the kitchen table and she took my hand in hers.

"I was also visited last night." Her eyes shone with joy.

"Bobby talked to you too?" I gasped.

She nodded. "I saw him laughing and playing with a bunch of other kids." She wiped a tear from her cheek with the palm of her hand. "He was running around and having a great time. He told me he was happy and there was nothing to worry about."

My heart began to mend that day. Years passed before I learned what happened to my sister the same night my brother visited mom and me. Seven years old at the time, she cried out in the night. When Mom checked on her and asked why she was crying, she said, "I saw Bobby."

Sixty years later, I still bear the scars of loss. The tears flow when I recall the horror of that fateful day. My throat tightens with sorrow when I talk about Bobby. Yet my heart glows with the undeniable knowledge that someday his hand will again nestle in mine.

A Shield From Danger

SUZAN KLASSEN

R odney, stop the car!"
As we drove down the road, my attention focused on the ramp leading to a busy interstate highway. A car was pulled off to the right side of the incline. The headlights of the zooming cars illumined a woman with dark hair in a black dress. I caught a glimpse of her confused face as she paced beside her car.

"That lady needs help, honey. We have to stop!"

My husband pulled over to the side of the road. But we were too far away to back up. Cars whipped past us.

I craned my neck for a better look. The lady continued to walk back and forth beside her car. It was a busy Friday night and many cars whizzed past her.

"Why in the world doesn't she get back in her car before she gets hit? We have to get to her quickly. She's in danger."

My husband studied the heavy traffic.

"Why aren't we backing up, Daddy?" our five-year-old demanded from the backseat.

"I can't back up. Why is it so important that we be the ones to help, anyway? Plenty of other people are out tonight. Surely someone else will stop."

"I don't know why. But *we* are the ones who are supposed to help," I insisted.

I started to pray out loud, "Dear Lord, please protect her. Get her in that car. Keep her safe till we can get back to her. Hide her from the view of the passing cars—people who might hurt her or take advantage of her—until we can get back there, and please slow down the traffic."

I glanced again over my shoulder. A man the size of a linebacker walked behind her. In the gleam of headlights, I saw that he had on a black shirt and light-colored slacks. His steps matched hers as he escorted her into her car.

Seeing a break in the traffic, my husband said, "I'll have to find a place to turn around."

As he drove off our son implored, "Aren't we going to help her?"

"Son, we'll go back. Give me time."

"Daddy, will we be there before anyone else?"

"I'm doing my best."

In order to distract my son, I said, "Michael, why don't you pray with me? 'Dear Lord, please help us make it back before anyone else stops. Clear out this traffic so we can help her safely. Keep her in her car. Make her stay put!'"

After several minutes, we arrived at the on-ramp again.

My husband pulled our car in behind hers and got out. He walked to her window. "What's wrong, ma'am?"

"My tire is flat. I think there's something wrong with the

rim too." She got out of the car and led him around to the passenger side. "See?" she said as she pointed at the back tire.

"Wow! Look at that tire rim. It's completely buckled. You must have smashed into the concrete edge of the ramp."

"Yes, I suppose I did."

"Do you have a spare tire?"

"Yes, I think so. Let me get my key for the trunk."

She handed my husband her key ring with the trunk key jutting out. He opened the trunk and took out the spare and the jack.

"My, she certainly is trusting. I don't think I would hand my keys over to a stranger," I said.

"Mommy, where is the big man?"

"I was wondering that myself. So you saw him too?"

"Yeah. He was really big!"

"Hmmm. Stay in the car, Michael. I'm going to talk to the lady."

"That tire rim looks pretty bad," I said to her.

"Yes," she said with a nervous laugh. "I prayed, 'God, you've got to send someone else to change this tire. It's beyond me. I need your help. Please send a Christian family to help me and keep me safe until they get here.'"

"So that's why we felt like we had to come back here. The pressure to help you was so intense even though you had that large man protecting you. Who was he, anyway? Where is he?"

She whirled to face me. "What man?"

"The large man with khaki slacks and a black shirt. He had a crew cut. He helped you get into your car. In fact, it seemed to me that he purposely blocked you from the view of passing cars."

My son called through the open window, "I saw him too."

147

"No one was here but me," she stammered, eyes wide. "God must have sent an angel to protect me. I asked Him to keep me safe." She broke into a smile. "God, you are so awesome!" She stretched her arms toward the sky.

My husband finished putting on the spare and pulled the jack out from under the car.

"Thank you so much, sir. I don't know what I would have done if you hadn't stopped."

We returned to our car and watched as she drove off.

Back on the road again, my husband said, "So you think maybe you saw an angel tonight?"

"Maybe. I can't think of another explanation. Michael and I both saw him, but no one was there except her when we arrived at her car. And she didn't even see him. It really did seem like he shielded her, the way he blocked her from the view of the other cars. Even his clothing seemed designed to protect her."

"His clothing? What do you mean?"

"Well, I know it's strange, but it was as if God wanted His angel to blend with what the woman was wearing, a black shirt and khaki slacks. She was wearing a black dress and her white legs really stood out. His black shirt matched her dress, and his khaki slacks hid her legs. It was almost like he made her invisible."

"Huh. Amazing to think about. So, why do you think God wanted us to help her? He could have just had the angel fix the flat."

"Maybe because He wanted us to be the answer to her prayer. She said she asked God to send her a Christian family."

"Really?"

"What I find interesting is that you never saw the man."

"Well if I had, I wouldn't have stopped."

"That's true. Maybe that's why you didn't see him, because God didn't let you. Strange, Michael and I both saw him, but we still thought we had to get back to her. I never once thought, 'Oh, good, there's a man there. He'll help her. We don't have to.' I was convinced that we had to be the ones."

I turned and looked at my son.

"Well, Michael, I think we got to be part of a miracle tonight. We saw God answer our prayers to protect that lady, and we were an answer to her prayer too."

He sat back in his seat and grinned.

An Amateur Exorcist

BOB HASLAM

When I boarded a plane on New Year's Eve to fly across the Pacific Ocean and around the world, I was traveling as an executive of an international relief organization, setting out to evaluate a variety of projects in the Philippines, Hong Kong, Thailand, Bangladesh, and India.

In the following days, during the height of the surge of boat people from Vietnam, I visited refugee camps in the Philippines, Hong Kong, and Thailand. I met people with heart-wrenching stories of how they'd barely survived Vietnamese army and navy gunfire and spent many hopeless days at sea without food or fresh water.

United States Navy ships had rescued many from boats that were not seaworthy. Others had crossed the border by land from Vietnam into Thailand.

I visited refugees in Bangkok in crowded camps and in cramped prisons. Many Vietnamese had crossed into Thailand not knowing they were required to register with local authorities before entering the country. As a result, they suffered the consequences in suffocating jails rather than in refugee camps.

In Bangladesh, people were destitute after floods caused by monsoon rains.

Desperation surrounded me everywhere I went. Our aid staff was busy going from village to village by boat distributing food and other supplies.

My next destination was India, where I spent time with aid workers in Calcutta, Bangalore, and Madras. In Madras, now known as Chennai, I visited a village rehabilitation project our relief agency had fully funded within the previous year.

The village, just outside of Madras, was a Hindu enclave located in a flood plain. Each year the homes were inundated by floodwaters in the heavy rainy season. Our Christian agency responded to the needs of this Hindu village by funding a major project to raise each home several feet. The space underneath was filled in with dirt and stones. Concrete was poured around the fill and above it, and concrete steps were built at the front of each home. When the annual rains came, the homes were now safely above flood level.

An Indian representative of our agency took me to visit the village. We walked on the gravel streets between elevated homes. People gathered into something of a parade as word spread that an American from the helpful relief agency was in their village. Many of them shook my hand and thanked me through the interpreter for the help they'd received.

This became a celebration as the crowd grew larger and noisier. I was treated with honor I had never experienced before. My interpreter kidded me that they were treating me as the populace had treated Mahatma Gandhi.

"Not so," I replied. "I'm wearing shoes and a safari suit. Gandhi walked barefoot dressed only in a loincloth."

What a humbling experience this turned out to be for me. Although I had helped raise funds for projects such as this, I had not been physically involved in carrying out the project. Yet these grateful people showered me with adulation.

The word spread from house to house about my walk through the village. Families poured out of their homes to join the procession.

But suddenly, the parade was stopped in its tracks. A man burst out of a house literally dragging his wife behind him. He pushed through the crowd and almost threw his wife at my feet.

The man spoke rapidly to my interpreter, glancing at me from time to time. When his speech was over, the interpreter told me the man was convinced that his wife was demon possessed. He said he had heard that Christ had cast out demons. He requested that I, as a representative of a Christian organization, cast the demon out of his wife.

The woman was on hands and knees on the gravel street at my feet, her face pointed toward the ground, her long hair dragging on the stones. The husband grabbed her hair and turned her face toward me.

I was appalled. The woman's face was contorted and her eyes wildly darted back and forth. She made no sound but seemed terribly afraid of me. Her husband pulled her up on her knees until her head was at my waist level.

"Please, please," he begged through the interpreter, "cast out this demon from my wife!"

I had never been in such a circumstance, but I had heard missionaries tell of casting out demons in the name of Jesus in African villages. I knew the Scriptures well and knew the power in the name of Jesus.

Silence now reigned as everyone strained to see and hear what I would do. The battle was staged before them as a Christian man was being asked to deliver a Hindu woman from demon possession.

I prayed inwardly for guidance and strength to respond to this woman's needs. Although I'd been tense, my spirit calmed. I knew what God wanted me to do. I'd heard stories of demons coming out of people with loud shrieks, but I had no idea what would happen next.

I laid both of my hands upon the woman's head. I felt her shaking violently as I began praying. I became aware that the interpreter was repeating my words in the villagers' language so the crowd could follow what was happening. I sternly commanded the evil spirit or spirits to come out of the woman in the name of Jesus Christ of Nazareth.

I completed my prayer with a resounding "Amen!"

Instantly, I noticed that the woman's shaking had stopped. When I removed my hands from her head, she turned her face upward, beaming with a beautiful smile. Her eyes were steady and clear. She stood to her feet as normal a person as anyone else in the crowd.

People around me began chattering and celebrating what they had seen happen before their very eyes. The interpreter kept up a running translation of what the villagers were saying. They were utterly amazed at the power of Jesus' name.

The husband shook my hand repeatedly with unbounded gratitude. I told him through the interpreter that Jesus was the one who had caused the change in his wife.

To my surprise, the man requested that I enter his home as his guest. He, his wife, my interpreter, and I climbed the cement steps into his home. For several minutes we carried on an animated conversation through the interpreter. Then he surprised me again.

"I ask you to please pray a prayer of blessing upon our home in the name of your Jesus," he said.

What an opportunity!

I talked aloud with the Lord, thanking Him for His act of kindness upon this man's wife. Then I asked the Lord to place a blessing upon the home and family.

When I said Amen and looked into their grateful smiling faces, I knew that this was the real reason I had made that trip around the world.

The Perfect Provider

CONNIE K. POMBO

M ark—please—come here!" I demanded.
"Just a minute . . . I'll be right there," my husband muttered in the other room.

"No, I need you now!" I shouted, hoping the neighbors wouldn't hear.

When Mark entered the bedroom, he found me holding a perfume bottle and surrounded by shards of glass.

"How in the world did you do that?" Mark blurted.

I burst into tears.

"It slipped out of my hands, landed on the dresser, and broke the glass in a million pieces." In between sobs I kept repeating, "I'm so sorry!"

As Mark cleaned up the glass around me—making a path so I could move out of the danger zone—I sobbed, "What are we going to do?"

Broken glass was no big deal—normally! But this was *not* our home and the antique glass top to the dresser was part of a treasured heirloom collection that belonged to the owners. We were house-sitting for a retired couple in Bradenton, Florida, while we waited for our departure date to Sicily, where we were to serve as missionaries.

We had given notice at our jobs, sold our cars, made plane reservations, and were hunkered down in a lovely three-bedroom home until we were scheduled to leave the States. What we hadn't planned on was a "natural" disaster!

After the glass was cleaned up and the white rug vacuumed, we assessed the damage. Mark ran his hands over the mahogany wood and announced, "This will be expensive to replace!"

I plopped on the bed and cried. "I think we need a glass angel!"

Sensing my desperation, Mark sat next to me and whispered, "Let's pray for one."

As Mark bowed his head, I secretly doubted how we could manage to pay for the glass replacement. We had no money, no car, barely enough food for the remaining two weeks, and we were sequestered in a home that wasn't ours.

The house we were staying in was part of a retirement community, and the owners were particular about their home: no children, no pets, and no messes. When we were handed the keys, we were given a lengthy "don't-do" list, which included no beverages in any part of the house except the kitchen. And we were given disposable "booties" to be worn at all times on the wall-to-wall *white* carpet. Most of the time—unless we were lying in bed—we stood at attention for fear we would accidentally spill or break something!

And now our worst nightmare had happened!

After Mark finished praying, he stood and announced, "We'll need to replace the glass!"

I nodded my head slowly.

After a few moments of awkward silence, I picked up the Saturday newspaper and spread it across the dresser to cut a pattern from its top. After paying careful attention to detail, I handed the pattern over to Mark so he could take it to the hardware store and get an estimate on the cost of glass cut just right for the dresser.

As soon as Mark slipped out the door, I carefully cleaned up the remaining glass, vacuumed the rug several times, and checked to make sure every shard was accounted for. Stepping on glass and getting blood on the white carpet was simply not an option.

As I put the remaining shards of glass in the garbage, the front door opened and Mark appeared with the glass estimate. He handed me the slip of paper and silently walked away.

I'm not sure what I expected, but $168 was certainly not in the ballpark!

I held up the paper and asked, "How will we ever pay for this?"

Mark slumped in the chair and didn't answer immediately. I watched as the frown—still stitched in his forehead—started to loosen.

Then he replied, "We'll have to call the Johnsons and let them know what happened. I'm sure they'll understand."

Mark picked up the phone and started to dial the number when I placed my hand over the receiver.

"What are you doing?" Mark questioned. "It's only right that we let them know."

"Uh-huh," I said with a shrug. "But can't we pray about it a little longer?"

Mark breathed in deeply and said, "Okay, but tomorrow after church we need to call."

"Of course!" I agreed.

The next morning—after a restless night's sleep—we prepared for the three-mile walk to church. As we crawled along in the heat and humidity, we kept silent. When we rounded the corner to the church, we could hear the guest pastor pounding on the pulpit and shouting, "And God will supply all your needs!"

He was a missionary to the Congo and continued to beat on the pulpit like a drum. A part of me wanted to turn back and head the other way, but Mark wrapped his arm around my waist and led me to the front row!

By the time the choir sang and the double doors of the church opened widely, I realized there was no choice but to accept our fate. We would have to call the Johnsons! We filed out of church—ignoring the sign for the all-church picnic— and walked home without a word.

When we approached the steps to the house, I broke the silence with an announcement. "I know . . . I can make muffins and sell them in the neighborhood and you can mow lawns. What do you think?"

Mark's eyes sparkled and a grin spread across his face. "That's great, honey! Except we don't have gas for the lawn mower, and you used the last of the flour to make pancakes last night."

My heart sank as Mark opened the door to the house, which was starting to feel more like a prison.

As soon as we stepped inside, Mark headed for the pristine living room to call the Johnsons, and I reached inside my purse to get their business card with the number on it.

When I opened my purse, I saw a small blank envelope that was unsealed. I opened it and saw a flash of green.

It was money—lots of money! Too surprised to speak, I started to count the bills—mostly twenties. When I reached the $100 mark, I let out a scream!

"Mark, look at this!" I shouted, as I held up the money. "It's all here—$168! We don't need to make that call."

It's been thirty years since the discovery of the $168 in my purse, and it still remains one of life's greatest mysteries. Not one person knew about the broken glass and no one had access to my purse. God supplied all of our needs—even though our faith was lacking. We left for Sicily on the scheduled departure date with all our debts paid!

How comforting to know that there are angels among us, and some of them are even assigned to help us replace glass!

Missiles With a Message

MIKE MCKOWN, as told to
ROBERT A. MCCAUGHAN

We were poised at the end of the runway, engines running, waiting to receive our final flight clearance, when the voice of the air traffic controller came over the radio: "Spectre 3, you are cleared for takeoff. After takeoff, right turn, climb and maintain 9,000 feet. . . . Be careful out there."

The sound of the four turbojet engines of our aircraft changed from whining to a roar as the pilot advanced the throttles. Then, as the brakes were released, the aircraft shuddered and moved forward, gathering speed.

The nose tilted upward. We were leaving Ubon Air Base, Thailand—headed for our target area—Laos, over the Ho Chi Minh Trail.

This particular day in the spring of 1972 was to be my last combat mission over Laos.

Our aircraft was an AC130A gunship, an airborne weapons system converted from a simple C130 transport designed to hunt and destroy targets on the ground. The gunship was very similar to the ones used in Afghanistan and Iraq today. It had two cannons and two Gatling guns mounted on the left side of the fuselage.

My job as Sensor Operator was to track enemy targets using the infrared system. The two rapid-firing, IR-guided Gatling guns were capable of destroying a cluster of enemy trucks and vehicles with a burst of gunfire lasting only a few seconds. Because of the horrific destructive capabilities of these gunships and the fright they caused the enemy, they were given the name Spectre.

Later that night, after completing our mission, we began our climb "out of the weeds," as we referred to leaving close-to-the-ground operations, and steered our aircraft toward home.

Right after we reached our assigned altitude, I heard a loud warbling sound in my headset. I felt a sudden rush of adrenalin as my stomach tightened with anxiety. It was the unmistakable audible warning of an imminent surface-to-air missile attack; an enemy SAM radar had locked onto our aircraft and was preparing to launch. This was terrifying as we were defenseless against a surface-to-air missile—without the ability to outrun, decoy, or shoot down a SAM.

I glanced over at the Electronic Warfare Officer seated next to me; he was intently looking at his electronic countermeasures equipment and the displays on his panel. Then I saw the yellow light that had come on only a moment ago turn red!

"We have a launch light!" the EWO said, his voice raising several octaves. Then another red light came on.

"We have a second launch!" he said, his voice even more stressed.

Suddenly, everything went quiet. Whereas a few seconds earlier our cockpit-interphone system was filled with idle chatter, comments, and profanity, now, apparently, every man was contemplating the threat at hand and the probability of certain death.

Everybody, most likely, is making his peace with God, I thought.

Then the voice of our Illuminator Operator, the crewman whose job it was to illuminate targets and get visual information from the ground, came over the interphone. Following standard procedure, he had looked out the back of the airplane to get a visual sighting on the SAMs. "I have the missiles in sight, and they are guiding beautifully," he said. His use of the word "beautifully" upset me terribly. For a moment I wanted to throw him out of the plane.

Well . . . this is it! I thought. I bowed my head and prayed: *Lord, I will be in your presence soon. . . . Please take care of my family.*

Hushed seconds went by; then a loud explosion occurred near the left side of our plane, buffeting us slightly—signaling that the first SAM had missed; not close enough to do damage. More quiet moments . . . then a second explosion high above us. A wave of relief swept over me as I brushed away the tears that had spotted my face. Both missiles had malfunctioned—missed us!

Thank you, Lord!

When we arrived back at Ubon, we were told by military intelligence that it was unlikely that we had experienced a SAM attack. If we had, we would all be dead; surface-to-air missiles don't malfunction, don't miss. However, several nights later at the same location, another Spectre gunship came under a SAM attack and was shot down; fourteen men were killed!

A few days later I received a letter from my wife, Norma. She had included in the envelope a church bulletin with a time written on it. She wrote that during the Sunday morning service, Dr. Bennet, our pastor, had suddenly interrupted the service and told them that they needed to stop immediately and pray for Mike McKown.

When I converted the Mountain Standard Time written on the church bulletin to local time in Laos, I realized that our church had stopped to pray for me at the exact time that those missiles were fired. Even to this day, when I think about it, I get goose bumps.

Well, God got my attention—in a big way. I realized that God had initiated and answered the prayers of His people. He had intervened and saved my life. I didn't understand it, but I knew one thing for sure: I belonged to God. Not only had He bought and paid for me at the cross, but He had demonstrated that He owned me, cared about me, and had further plans for my life on this earth. Before I used to think of God and me as riding a tandem bike. I would steer, and God would pedal from behind. Now I realized I had it all wrong. I needed to trust Him to steer, and I needed to pedal and follow His lead.

I have to confess that when I decided to trust Jesus as Lord, I feared I would be sent as a missionary to some remote place in Africa. Instead, God sent our family to Solano County, California, where I now serve Him as a Gideon, volunteer jail chaplain, and of course in our church.

God got my attention. He *is* Lord!

Enemy at the Door

JANE OWEN

T hank you, Lord, for setting a guard around our home,"
I murmured.

Against the coal-black sky, a cooling breeze ruffled
the fronds of the coconut palms in our yard in St. Marc, Haiti.
They swayed like eerie, dancing figures keeping watch over us.

As my husband, Ron, and I tucked our children into bed,
we prayed for their safety and a peaceful night's sleep. Three-
year-old Leah hugged her bear and went to sleep quickly.
Eleven-month-old Aaron was restless. Jo, a friend who was
visiting from the States, picked him up.

"I need to rock this sweet boy," she said. Aaron nestled
into her arms.

"Jo, I'll take my shower while you hold Aaron."

The cold water refreshed me, and over the gentle blasts of

water, I enjoyed hearing the soothing sounds of Jo's singing interspersed with prayers for our son.

I finished bathing and checked on my contented, sleeping boy.

"You have the touch, Grandma Jo."

She chuckled. "He's a precious baby."

While Ron was taking his turn in the shower, Jo and I went outside to look at the stars in the clear night sky. The full moon was rising like a huge balloon over the mountains.

Suddenly, the peace was rent by a cacophony of noise. Shouting. Shrieking! Rhythmic drums! Blaring horns!

It was another Rah Rah season.

Jo looked down the road at the mass of people coming our way. "Isn't Rah Rah what these folks celebrate in place of Lent?"

"Yes." I had explained to her that this twisted practice originated in the early days of Papa Doc Duvalier's rule over Haiti. He had dedicated the island of Haiti to Satan and declared voodoo the official religion.

Jo shook her head. "What an ungodly legacy this country has."

I put my arm around her shoulder. "Let's go inside."

We climbed the steps to the second floor, watching out the middle bedroom window.

"Look at those poor people," Jo said. "What a monstrous commotion."

This was her first time to witness Haiti's demonic display. Some people carried lanterns. Swinging them, they followed their witch doctor chanting discordant songs.

Red and black paint covered the witch doctor's face and arms. His bare upper torso had an oily sheen, and he wore a horned headdress.

Jo trembled. "That gives me chills."

Just then lantern light lit his face.

"Jane, his eyes are wild!"

"Our Haitian friends told us he uses several kinds of drugs to lead this praise fest for Satan."

We both jumped when the witch doctor cracked his bull-whip. Moving grotesquely down his line of followers, he snapped the leather rope violently over their heads.

Ron stepped into the room.

"You ladies don't have to watch what the devil's doing," he said.

"You're right," I agreed. "I think they're going on into town, thank the Lord."

Ron and I checked our sleeping children and we all went downstairs.

As we sat sipping fresh orange juice, Jo asked, "Are you and Ron used to this devil worship?"

"I can't ignore its reality," I said. "It can still be unsettling."

"We've experienced encounters beyond our imagination," Ron added. "It's hard to see people in such bondage."

"The first time a witch doctor brought his Rah Rah group to our front gate a couple of years ago, Ron was preaching at a church in another town," I recalled. "They came with all that horrible clanging and banging. I started praying. The Lord told me to play 'The Hallelujah Chorus' on our cassette player. So I turned up the volume and said, 'Satan, here's some real praise music for you!'"

"What did they do?" asked Jo.

"They quickly took their party elsewhere," I answered.

The three of us sat silently while insects buzzed the room's single light bulb.

"Tell Jo about the time Jesus protected Leah at the market," Ron said.

Jo leaned forward. "What happened?"

I took a deep breath. "We had been here for about three weeks when Carol, another missionary, invited me to go to the open market in the heart of town. I took Leah with me and met Carol halfway. She greeted me with, 'Why did you bring Leah?'

"I asked what she meant. 'Someone may try to take her from you,' she told me. 'You'd better hold her in your arms when we get to the market area.'

"I was stunned; then I thought of Psalm 34:7 and said, 'Carol, the angel of the Lord is camped about us. We're not going to be afraid.'

"When we finished shopping in the open area, Leah wanted to get down. Since Carol asked to visit one more shop, I continued to hold Leah. It was a tiny space, and inside the air smelled like something spoiled. When I caught a glimpse of a woman pushing through a crowd of people directly toward us, I tightened my arms around my daughter. The woman came at me, reaching for Leah.

"She started chanting, 'You give me your baby! You give me your baby!'

"I shook my head and turned away. She pulled at my arms.

"'In the Name of Jesus, take your hands off my baby!' I shouted.

"Her eyes widened and she ran away. This whole time, Leah never even stiffened in my arms, but kept her head pressed to my chest. I know the Lord kept her little heart at ease."

"God is so good," Ron added. "Without His protection, we couldn't live here—we wouldn't live here."

"That's for sure," I agreed. "Did I ever tell you about Leah's vision?"

"This was amazing," Ron interjected. "We had been here about a month, and Leah was twenty months old . . ."

I picked up the account. "We were sitting in the rocking chair singing 'Jesus Loves Me.' Leah sat straight up and pointed across the room.

"'Look, Mommy!' she said. 'There's a man!'

"'Where?' I asked. I thought someone had come into the house.

"'He's right over there. Mommy, he's *gro*! He's *belle*!'

"I didn't know she knew the Creole words for *big* and *beautiful*."

"The next week," Ron continued, "she saw him again. She acted like it was nothing unusual."

"She just looked at the doorway and with a big grin said, 'That pretty man is back,'" I said.

"She saw an angel or the Lord himself!" said Jo. "That's also why she wasn't afraid at the market."

I finished my orange juice and paused. "I'd like to tell you about another experience. The Lord used it to teach us about standing against the demonic forces here."

Jo drew her shawl around her shoulders. The night air was chilly, yet it was still—too still. She waited for me to continue.

"I was a couple months pregnant with Aaron. Ron and I had put Leah down for the night; then, although it was early, we went to bed. We were homesick for our families . . ."

Ron chimed in, "We knew God led us to Haiti but didn't understand why—"

"What was that?" I interrupted him, as I saw something move outside the window. Strangely, it vibrated the screen and was gone.

"It's probably the wind, Jane." Ron tilted his head. "Go ahead with what happened that night."

"As I said, we were in bed and had begun to pray. All of a sudden, I couldn't breathe. Someone or something was choking me. I sat up and realized Ron was struggling too. He was gasping, 'Jesus!'

"I felt two hands clenched about my throat. We were battling a force not of this world. I'll never forget hearing myself croak, 'Jesus! Jesus!'"

"When it was over, we were exhausted," Ron said.

"But," I said, "His Name kept us safe."

Ron stretched and yawned. "Let's head up to bed on that note."

We went up the steps, and Jo said, "I'll check on the children."

As she passed our bedroom she whispered, "They're sleeping like little lambs. See you in the morning." Ron and I got into bed. Soon he was snoring. I started drifting off, but in a split second I was wide awake.

Something wasn't right.

My body tensed. I heard a door close.

Was that Jo's door?

As I stared into the hallway, a horrible being glided up the stairs! It was hunched over and floated. Panic crept up my spine. The smell was awful, like a smoldering fire.

Horrified, I watched this dark thing move toward the children's room. I shook Ron awake.

"Something! Something is . . ." I spoke in rasping tones as I scrambled to Leah and Aaron.

Ron sprang out of bed. "Help us, Jesus!"

Ron pushed the children's door. It was ajar but wouldn't move to open any more. My mouth was dry, my lips parched. I swallowed hard.

Ron pushed again. It opened, and we found our two darlings, still sleeping. Ron searched the closet and under Leah's bed. Then he went to the door leading to the patio off the hallway. It was locked. Opening it, he saw nothing, but that smell hung in the air.

"It must have passed through here," Ron said. "Praise God, it couldn't stay!"

We took turns sleeping the rest of the night, thanking the Lord for His protection.

The next morning, Jo came to breakfast and announced, "The devil tried to scare me last night."

I looked at Ron. "Did you see something, Jo?"

"I saw an ugly creature come up the steps."

"What did it look like, Jo?" I asked.

"It was a dark beast—all crouched over, moving like curtains fluttering in the wind." She hesitated. "It brushed my arm as I walked into my bedroom."

Jo looked at Ron. "Did you see it?"

"No, but I could smell it," he said. "The odor was terrible, like heavy smoke."

Jo studied us. "The Lord told me it came for the children."

"It did," I said. "Several Haitian friends warned us to be vigilant, especially for Leah and Aaron."

"Why didn't you call me?" Jo demanded.

"We thought you were sleeping," I said. "Everything was racing in high gear."

"And we didn't want to alarm you," added Ron.

"It's odd I didn't hear you." She stirred her coffee. "After I saw that demon, I prayed on through the night."

Just then Leah came downstairs. She wore a big smile as she climbed up on Jo's lap.

"Aaron's up too," she said with a giggle.

I knew God had kept us all safe. The power of trusting Him was stronger than the most threatening face of fear. Looking around the table at my loved ones, I said, "The enemy might muster a strong attack . . . but God's protection is stronger!"

The Locked Room Mystery

Jonathan Reiff

O n graduation day in June 1960 I was ready to face the world, and that very afternoon with a "Yes, Sir!" I reported for duty in the U.S. Army.

I had majored in International Politics under Dr. Henry Kissinger at Harvard.

My father, Dr. Harry Reiff, was the professor of International Law at St. Lawrence University in Canton. His parents were German Russian immigrants who had discouraged him from going to college. Despite his parents' objections, my dad worked hard and received a scholarship to Harvard University. Naturally he wanted his sons—my brother, Daniel, and me—to have the same fine education.

Besides majoring in International Politics, I'd enrolled in the ROTC program. So that summer I attended Officers

Training, Ranger School, and Paratrooper School at Fort Benning, Georgia, and was excited about serving my country as an army officer. After completing the training, I was assigned to a tank division in West Germany.

On August 15, 1961, the East Germans closed East Berlin and began building the Berlin Wall. The closing divided the city of Berlin into two parts: two-thirds West Berlin and one-third East Berlin.

A large number of us servicemen were transferred to Berlin that very day to help defend the city in case the East Germans or the Russians attacked it. The 10,000 American soldiers serving in Berlin were called The Berlin Brigade.

Checkpoint Charlie was a famous crossing point where the Russians prevented Americans from going into East Berlin. At that time many people who wanted freedom from the Communists in East Berlin tried dramatic escapes: trucks crashing through the Berlin Wall, small cars sneaking under the checkpoints when the guards weren't looking, tourist boats filled with those wanting to escape down the river, people climbing over high tension wires, and others jumping out of upper windows to escape to West Berlin.

The city of Berlin was fifty miles across with forests and lakes, and the American Army trained in those forests. Serving as a lieutenant, an infantry officer, I participated in a number of military exercises throughout the fall and winter.

One cold week during the winter, we were on a special training maneuver in the forest, preparing to defend Berlin. During that whole week we slept outside in sleeping bags in the snow.

In the middle of the week I realized I was very sick. I could hardly eat, so I drank huge quantities of milk for energy. I was very achy during the maneuvers, but because I was an officer and the exercise was my duty, I continued the effort all day long and often all through the night.

At night we went on hard, long-distance foot patrols. Because I had eaten very little, I was weak and lost weight. My uniform hung on me. But I didn't tell anyone how bad I felt. I decided that after the maneuvers were over, I'd go get checked out by a doctor.

On returning to the military post in Berlin Friday night, my company was put on alert to go out with a tank company to confront the Russians, who had blocked the superhighway into Berlin. It was potentially a combat duty. I knew if we were called to do it, we would go out on Saturday morning with tanks equipped with bulldozer blades. If necessary, we'd push the Russian tanks off the highway they were blockading.

I knew that if we were assigned to this, it would be my duty to go with my soldiers, so I chose not to go to the hospital that night. I was dead tired, so exhausted I could hardly move. I returned to my officers' quarters and went directly to bed.

We bachelor officers lived in concrete buildings with thick steel doors on our apartments. We opened those heavy doors with a key and they locked automatically upon closing.

In the middle of the night I got up to use the bathroom and passed out. When I woke up, I was lying on my back in the hall with sharp pain on my left side. Several times I tried to get up, but each time I lifted my head, I passed out before I could move. Because of the severe pain in my left shoulder, I thought I'd suffered a heart attack.

I figured that since I passed out every time I moved my head, any moment might be my last moment of consciousness, so I had to get help quickly. I remained on my back and pushed myself with my feet down the hall to the living room, where the phone sat on a table.

Since I couldn't reach the phone, I pulled it down by the cord and hoped it didn't break. I succeeded in pulling the phone down and caught it! The room was dark and I couldn't see, so I had to figure out how to dial both letters and numbers on a rotary dial without being able to see them.

It took some time, but fortunately I was able to remember my friend Lieutenant Bob Sands's number and successfully dialed it. When he answered, I said, "Bob, I need you to come get me and take me to the hospital. I think I've had a heart attack."

About fifteen minutes later, Bob rushed into the apartment. He carried me to his car and zoomed straight to the hospital. The doctors discovered I had a ruptured spleen the size of a football and operated immediately. After spending four months in the hospital and in rehab, I was able to return to duty as an army officer.

How can you explain that on the night when I desperately needed immediate help, Bob could walk right into my apartment? Right through a heavy steel casement door that was always locked?

If Bob had not been able to open that heavy door, I probably would have died in a short time. The only other key was in the engineers' headquarters elsewhere in Berlin. And it was unlikely the duty officer could have gotten the key on a Friday night when many soldiers were out on the town.

Is there any other explanation but that God sent an angel to unlock that heavy steel door that Friday night in Berlin?

I believe there is no other way to explain how I survived that ordeal and am alive today.

A Face Needing Forgiveness

Anneliese Jawinski, as told to
Ingrid Shelton

When I woke up early one morning, something seemed to be wrong. A strange feeling flowed through me. I became aware that I was slowly rising, but my body stayed behind on the bed.

My eyes focused on the light bulb in the center of the ceiling. A face glowing in the light looked back at me. It was the face of my mother.

Instantly I began to shake. Was this a nightmare? No, I knew this was real life, not just a dream. Intense fear swept through me.

"But my mother is dead!" I cried out terrified. "Did she come to get me? Am I leaving this earth now? Oh, God, please, I don't want to go yet. I still have so much to accomplish," I pleaded.

"You haven't forgiven your mother," a quiet voice announced.

"I thought I'd forgiven her," I answered weakly. "It was only a few months ago, but I did. I forgave her."

A flash of sorrow and guilt swept through me even as I spoke those words.

When I was thirteen years old, in January 1945, I had left my home in Poland. My father had died when I was three years old and my mother had remarried. Neither my four brothers nor I liked my stepfather. He seemed to be especially cruel to my brothers, beating them while my mother stood by and didn't even try to stop him.

Didn't my mother care? I had wondered. *Why did she allow this beating when my brothers hadn't done any wrong?* Even though my stepfather did not abuse me physically, my heart ached for my brothers, so I spent a lot of time at my grandmother's home nearby or with my best friend's family. They gave me the love I did not get at home.

My two oldest teenage brothers had been drafted into the German army. My third brother had also left home to live at a youth camp. Only my youngest brother, Edmund, was still at home with me. Now there was no way I wanted to stay at home any longer.

"I am leaving too," I told Edmund. "Please, come with me. Let's stay together," I pleaded, but he was afraid.

"Well, then I'm going alone," I told him. Hatred for my mother filled my heart, and I couldn't get away fast enough. At first I went to live with a friendly couple I knew in a nearby town. They took me in as their own daughter, and I felt cared for.

Yet I soon realized I could not stay there permanently. Within weeks the Russian army came close to our area, and

I could hear heavy artillery. I was afraid of the Russians, so I wanted to get away before they overran our town.

A fifteen-year-old girl next door also wanted to head west to Germany, so we decided to leave immediately. Just the day before, Jack, a seventeen-year-old boy, had arrived at her house. He had been conscripted by the German army but had deserted his post.

"I will help you get to Germany," he offered. "I know of ways to get you out of here. But please, keep my past a secret, otherwise a Nazi army official will shoot me."

We helped him bury his army clothes in the back of the garden. Then we packed a change of clothes into a little backpack and walked to the train station. Trains ran only occasionally, and all of them were packed with retreating German soldiers fleeing from the pursuing Russian army. We decided to start walking west, following the train tracks. I was small for my age and tired easily. Jack often carried me on his back.

Jack always listened for a train heading west. When one came along, he showed us how to jump underneath the train cars. We soon became adept at jumping on moving trains. Jack also knew where to find food left behind in homes deserted by their owners.

Three days later we arrived at the main Berlin train station in Germany and parted ways. A Red Cross worker took me to a kind farm family who treated me like a daughter. I often thought of my brothers, but I did not miss my mother. I still felt bitter toward her, put her out of my mind, and lost all contact with her.

Over the years I found each of my four brothers, and we kept in touch. I never tried to find my mother. *She didn't care about me, so why should I care about her?* I told myself.

A few years later I married, and in 1955 my new husband and I immigrated to Canada. Years went by. One day, my youngest brother, Edmund, told me how my mother had missed me after I had left.

"She cried herself to sleep many nights, hoping that you would somehow contact her," he said. "She wanted to know if you were all right. She wanted you to know she was sorry that she had kept her feelings to herself. And she blamed herself for driving you away from home. She wanted to see you so badly, especially before she died."

The bitter feelings toward my mother began to evaporate somewhat when I heard of my mother's last days. I finally realized that she did not know how to show love, that she had cared about me, but she had tried to please her new husband.

"Oh, I forgive you, Mom," I whispered when I passed by her photo I had finally put up on the mantel of my home. The words hadn't really come from my heart, but they made me feel better.

Now, as I was suspended in midair, the look on my mother's sad face reflected in the ceiling light sent shivers down my back.

"You have not really forgiven her. You just said the words. You need to forgive her with your heart and soul." I heard the voice a second time.

Pain shot through me as I realized my forgiveness had not been genuine.

"God, I forgive her. I really do!" I cried. "But, please, let me live to continue my work on earth," I begged.

I did not hear the voice again, but I instantly felt drawn back into my body and knew I would live. Right away I jumped up from my bed and ran to the mantel to look at my mother's picture. Suddenly, I saw her in a different light.

I remembered what my brother Edmund had told me about my mother.

"Mom, I forgive you. I forgive you with all my heart," I said over and over. For a few minutes I just stood there looking at her photo, tears pouring down my face, my heart reaching out in love. Then a peace filled my soul, and I felt free, as if a burden had been lifted from my heart.

When I went back to the bedroom, my mother's face had vanished from the ceiling lamp.

Why did God allow me to see my mother's face? I wondered. *Was it so that I could learn to forgive the way God forgives?*

Whatever the reason, today I look forward to seeing my mother again in eternity and spending time with her in a loving relationship.

Fresh Wind of Peace

LORETTA J. EIDSON

The pastor told me to pray wherever I'd like. A couple of people were walking around, praying silently. One person was facedown on the floor, while others knelt in different places praying out loud.

I spotted a corner at the front left of the church near where an open archway led to the baptistry. It looked like the perfect spot for me pray.

En route to my chosen area, I thought about the vandalism the church had experienced during a construction project. It had stopped for a while, but recently the damage had become disturbing. Red spray paint on the new brick blasted foul language and threats. Leftover bricks were broken and roofing supplies stolen.

Just a few days before this prayer meeting was scheduled, a Bible was discovered in the church mailbox shredded to pieces. I was stunned as I tried to grasp the amount of hatred it must take to destroy a Bible. It bothered me to think that Satan could gain such control over people that they would deface church property and disrespect God's Word.

When I reached my corner of the sanctuary, I opened my Bible to Ephesians 6 and prayerfully read about God's armor. Then I set my Bible down on the front pew and began praying. The dim lights made the setting perfect for an intense time of prayer. As I talked to the Lord, I paced back and forth near the archway.

A Bible passage from the book of James came to my mind: *"Resist the devil, and he will flee from you."*

So I began resisting Satan and commanding him to stop his attacks against the church. I prayed for protection for God's property and the surrounding area. I quoted more Scriptures as they came to my mind and prayed more fervently. I prayed for deliverance and salvation for those who had caused so much damage.

After approximately thirty minutes of pacing and praying, I began feeling I should go through the archway into the shadows. A strange heaviness came over me as I felt the need to tell Satan that this church belonged to God and that he was trespassing on God's property.

I took about five steps beyond the archway and was about to tell Satan that he was evicted when intense fear tried to consume me. I resisted the fear and began praying for God's direction, wisdom, and discernment. Why was I experiencing fear in the church? Goose bumps popped up all over my body.

Praying wasn't anything new to me. I'd been involved in special prayer meetings for a couple of years and had encountered many different situations. I'd prayed for people with marriage problems, teenager problems, work problems, and esteem problems. Even though I had prayed for God to deliver people from being oppressed and attacked by evil spirits, I still wasn't quite ready for what was about to happen.

Without warning, something grabbed my throat and began choking me. I could feel the tight squeeze, which instantly made me stop praying. My eyes watered profusely. I swung my arms and hands helplessly, trying to fight whatever or whoever had such a powerful hold on my throat.

No one was there to grab.

I tried to run back into the openness of the sanctuary, but my feet didn't seem to touch the floor. I gurgled the name of Jesus. Immediately, my feet hit the floor.

When I ran out through the archway, several members of the prayer team were running toward me. They had heard growling.

I didn't.

I sat down to catch my breath. Wiping the tears from my face, I tried to make sense of what had just happened. The area through the archway hadn't been that dark. I could actually see pretty clearly, until my throat was grabbed and my eyes blurred. No doors were open and no windows were accessible. The space beyond the archway appeared to be empty.

The team gathered around me and prayed God's protection over me. As I prayed quietly with them, I kept my eyes on that archway. I tried to visualize what that demon might have looked like. It felt so powerful and left me feeling so helpless and defeated.

I was disheartened. I had never felt a physical, though invisible, touch from a demon before. I didn't like it.

Since the rest of the group had heard a growl coming from beyond the archway, we agreed we were dealing with the demonic. We asked God to intervene in this situation and to give us wisdom to know exactly what to do. Another prayer time was scheduled for Friday night, which would give us three days to fast.

When I arrived home, I tucked my children into bed for the night and went to my bedroom. My husband was working a twenty-four-hour shift, so I was alone in my room. As I lay there rehashing the prayer meeting, I decided to turn the light back on and read my Bible. I needed encouragement from God.

Almost instantly the hair on my arms and neck stood straight up. Goose bumps crawled up and down my spine. I felt an evil presence enter my room. I didn't see anything. I didn't hear anything. I felt the eeriness of evil.

My thoughts reeled as my mind began hearing all types of accusations.

You have no power over Satan—you don't read your Bible enough, you don't pray enough, and you are a nobody. You make mistakes, and you are a useless part of that prayer team. You couldn't even defeat Satan's attack tonight.

Remembering that the Bible talks about Satan being a liar and a thief, I recognized his tactics to intimidate me and keep me from following through with fasting and prayer. I gripped my Bible, placed my right hand on the open pages, and prayed for wisdom. As I looked around my empty bedroom, I resisted the devil in Jesus' name and commanded him and his demons to leave my bedroom and my home.

Slowly, the goose bumps faded and the hair on my arms and neck began to relax. I prayed again, thanking God for rescuing me. I praised God for giving His children authority over the enemy.

I got out of bed, checked on my children, and walked through my house, singing praises to God. My home felt as if a fresh wind had blown through and left peace. My children were sound asleep, and my heart rejoiced. I felt victory over the attack of the enemy. I went back to bed and slept with my Bible tucked under my arm.

When Friday arrived and everyone gathered to pray, we focused on the area beyond the archway.

The pastor felt that since he was the spiritual leader of the church, he should walk inside the designated area while the rest of the team prayed.

We prayed for about forty-five minutes before the pastor walked through the archway. In moments he came wobbling out with his eyes closed and fell to the floor shaking. We intensified our praying. I wondered if we should call 9-1-1.

I grabbed my Bible and read out loud Luke 10:19 where Jesus said, "I have given you authority to trample on snakes and scorpions and to overcome all the power of the enemy; nothing will harm you."

I then turned to Philippians 2:10–11: "At the name of Jesus every knee should bow, in heaven and on earth and under the earth, and every tongue acknowledge that Jesus Christ is Lord, to the glory of God the Father."

Almost instantly, the pastor stopped shaking and gurgling. He opened his eyes, rubbed his throat, and began breathing normally.

I was so relieved. I wondered how we could explain such an incident to the police.

The pastor got back on his feet, smiled, and began praising the Lord. He said he took authority over the demonic presence and told it to leave the property in Jesus' name. Satan had to bow his knee. He had to go.

The pastor turned on some praise music and we all marched through the sanctuary declaring God's total deliverance for our church.

We marched circles in and out of the archway several times with no disruptions, hindrances, or incidents. We were so excited. God was victorious.

As our prayer time ended, an overwhelming peace and assurance engulfed me. My faith was increased as a new sense of confidence in God's deliverance and power was planted deep within my heart.

The Glimmering Gown

CONNIE BROWN

I brushed a strand of mousy brown hair from my eyes, bit my lower lip, and wiped the kitchen counter again. My husband's best friends from college would be over for dinner at any moment.

I'd been cooking, cleaning, and chasing kids all day in preparation. How did so many fingerprints get everywhere? Why hadn't we painted the house? I hoped the Martins wouldn't notice the spots on the carpet.

Two children charged through the kitchen with a barking cocker spaniel in pursuit. The doorbell rang. I covered the casserole and shoved it back in the oven.

Lord, please help this evening go well.

I felt covered with sweat and worries, but I forced a smile. I hoped to sit down soon and catch my breath.

Ready or not . . .

We hadn't seen David's college friends since we'd moved to another state fifteen years earlier. That was long before children started filling our home and lives with a menagerie of pets, projects, clutter, and laughter.

After I welcomed John and Sara Martin into our home, their two children and our four were instant friends. I envied them their ease. I had always felt shy and nervous around people I didn't know well. I was relieved when David finally got home so he could do most of the talking while I finished in the kitchen. David was excited to see them again. He had even come home early from his demanding job for the first time in weeks.

The Martins were taking an extended road trip, visiting relatives and old friends as they traveled from California to the East Coast. They had worked long hours in their home-based business before they sold it. Now they were taking a much-needed vacation, driving across country in a motor home and stopping to stay with family and friends on their way. That weekend was our turn to host them in our Colorado home.

While the Martins talked, John smiled often at Sara or grabbed her slender hand or waist. I crammed my worn nails into my jeans pockets and went to check on the casserole. Taking care of four active children, pursuing night classes, and doing volunteer work at church and the local elementary school left me little time for trips to the beauty or nail salon.

When dinner was ready, we fed the children first and then settled them in front of a movie in the family room so we could keep talking uninterrupted.

While we ate by candlelight, David and his two college friends quickly caught up with each other's lives. Soon they began talking about pranks and stories from four years of campus life together. I listened, smiled, and nodded from time to time. David and I had met after they'd graduated. Most of their memories were new to me.

"Just think what might have happened if you'd picked Sara instead of Carla that night on our first double date," John said. "Instead, here we are. And I've got the best wife ever."

Sara's cheeks turned an attractive pink as both men beamed their admiration. David didn't think to say something nice about me in return. He was the take-the-trash-out type and not so quick with romantic words.

I wish I could say I took my husband's silence in stride while both men admired Sara and then launched into another story. But my self-worth was at a low point that year while I was trying to raise children, lose weight, and complete a college degree. David and I had been fighting a lot about his overtime hours, the kids, and finances. David hadn't looked at me as he was looking at Sara in a long time. Something about that moment pierced into a deep, hurting place in my heart.

I picked up several empty plates, retreated to the kitchen, and began to wash them. My long hair covered misting eyes. David offered to help when he brought more dishes to the counter, but I waved him back to his friends. Eventually the three college buddies went to check on the kids and settle them into pajamas and sleeping bags.

Misty eyes were becoming mini-streams, so while they were busy with the kids, I escaped to our bedroom to pray. I crawled under the covers. Ten minutes, maybe fifteen passed, and I still didn't feel ready to face anyone. I just wanted to hide. How could I serve dessert when I only wanted to cry?

Lord, help me.

Eventually I heard David and the Martins talking in the

living room. I knew I couldn't avoid them much longer. I struggled to my feet.

I felt like the foster child I'd been in my early years—someone who could never really belong with the laughing people at the dinner table, who wasn't good enough.

Light streamed through our bedroom window. I stood in it, looking out at the Rocky Mountains. Starlight illuminated the Colorado prairie and distant snow-capped peaks. I didn't want to leave the sight. It was beautiful.

Lord, I'm sorry. You've brought me so far from a troubled childhood and hand-me-down dresses. You've given me a husband who loves me . . . and children . . . and a home. You've helped me so often. Help me again to do what's right. Help me serve you and others, here, now.

I lingered in the starlight a moment longer, breathing slowly. Before I could force myself to go back to our guests and be hospitable, I felt something light float over me. I began to feel as though I wore a glimmering evening gown more beautiful than anything I'd ever seen on a movie star or Cinderella.

I looked down. I couldn't see the gown, yet I could feel it, and it felt amazing. I felt beautiful in it and rich. I felt clean, valued, loved. I wasn't an awkward, scruffy kid. For the first time, I felt like a child of a King.

This must be what it feels like to wear Christ, I thought as I rinsed my face and eyes. And I could smile. Even my eyes could smile. God *had* answered my prayer.

I think I half glided around the house the rest of the evening as I served cake and coffee. I even joined in the friendly banter now and then.

Since that evening I've sometimes prayed to have the heart to see myself covered in that beautiful gown again. Although I haven't been able to see it, I know now God can.

I'm amazed that regardless of our hurts and troubles, past or present, God sees His children as beautiful. He sees us dressed in the shimmering light and textures of Christ's elegance. When I remember this, my chin rises ever so slightly.

And when I step out to serve Him and others, even my eyes smile.

Beyond the Fear of Death

KRISTIN H. CARDEN

S weat poured off of the operating table. I was aware of distant frantic voices and someone sitting me up to rip the gown from my body.

I could hear the heart monitor's beeping going wild. I was on fire. I was only sixteen years old. I was having a routine operation to fix a broken nose. But I felt like I was going to die.

Soon I was clinically dead.

As a young child, I had fears. I was scared of the dark. I was scared of fireworks. I was scared of being alone.

These are fears that many children wrestle with. My parents would pray over me and comfort me with Scripture, but I was still haunted by fear.

As I grew older, my fears intensified. I was becoming handicapped by fear. My fear of death sucked the air from my lungs with just a thought. Of course I was afraid to lose anyone I loved, but I was even more afraid for myself. The great unknown caused many nights of tossing and turning with anxiety. Even my belief in heaven brought little comfort. I felt swallowed up by the thought of eternity.

Playing or attempting to play sports was not a good match for a kid like me. I was perpetually in my own world of imagination. In that world I felt safe and did not experience fear.

However, there is no escaping sixth-grade phys ed. The day came when we had to play softball. I placed myself in the outfield so I could leisurely explore my imagination. Unfortunately, my team suffered for that because I missed the fly ball that landed somewhere to my left.

My phys ed teacher blew her whistle and loudly called me toward her. She tersely reminded me that a key component to softball was keeping your eye on the ball. She then asked me to stay close by and take the position of catcher.

Once again, I missed my opportunity, and somehow my face got in the way of a bat. The force of the practice swing that my cheek connected with pushed me back to the bleachers, where I dropped like a rock.

I roused to see my classmates and teacher surrounding me in a haze. My exasperated teacher sent me to the front office for an ice pack. She didn't realize that I had cracked my cheekbone and had a concussion. Needless to say, I returned to school the following day with orders from my mother to be excused from phys ed.

I was glad for the break; I could go to my happy place. However, my teacher planted me at the top of the bleachers with clear instructions to "practice keeping your eye on the ball."

I thought I was keeping my eye on the ball. But out of

nowhere, it landed square on my nose, causing me to fall off of the bleachers.

It was not a good day.

My broken nose made breathing hard and life just more difficult for a kid who was already awkward. I suffered with this affliction for four years before the powers that be finally decided I needed surgery.

I was terrified of the surgery, but I hated my broken nose even more. I was assured and reassured that this was a simple, routine procedure and I would even go home the same day to recover in my own bed, with my mom ready to pamper me.

When the day arrived, I begged for more reassurance from the nurse as she prepped me for surgery. She seemed amused by my worry. Of course it would be fine. It was really no big deal. I had nothing to fear.

Sometime later, the heat woke me up. My skin was burning.

I started screaming that I was on fire. My lungs were craving air.

As the frantic efforts of the medical team continued, I prayed for relief. I cried out for help.

Then in an instant, it all stopped. The fire was replaced with the sweetest sensation on my skin, along with a euphoria I can't really describe in words. It seemed like my whole body was filled with light and every cell and nerve was able to perceive it.

I could see myself on the operating table and the doctors and nurses scrambling in panic. In the distance I heard the one long beep that comes with a flat line on the monitor. What impacted me more than anything, though, was that I had no fear. I felt complete comfort and safety. I felt no shame or sorrow in seeing my body lifeless on that table. I felt more connected to myself than I ever had, before then or since.

It would be nice to say that I had a glorious vision of the streets of gold or that I saw Jesus or met Paul. But I did hear a voice say, "It's not time."

Strangely, I believe I felt disappointed. I have sometimes thought that heaven itself must be even further from explanation because this little taste of glory was delicious.

I woke up seeing my mother's face. Her worried expression relaxed into relief as I looked at her.

For the next few days I couldn't talk about my experience, though I relived it over and over in my mind. Finally, I was able to discuss it with my parents. They were still frightened by my close call.

I was thankful for the experience. I had a firsthand taste of death and found it not so scary after all. I was able to hear my Father's voice, I believe, reassuring me that He knows the time when I will come to Him—and when it's not time, well, it's not time. He wiped away all my fears in an instant of cool relief.

This experience has been a benchmark for me, to remind me that fear keeps us in bondage. When we are slaves to fear, we truly are wrapped in chains. We aren't able to experience the freedom that Jesus paid for in His death. He conquered death so that we might truly live.

Now I have children who wrestle with fear. I am so thankful that I can address these fears with a deeper perspective of God's sovereignty. I find a great deal of peace in knowing that His will and timing are perfect.

The Lord knows us. He knows that fear plagues us, and that is why He tells us over and over again in His Word, "Do not fear."

We have sung the words to Isaiah 43 every night to our children since they were very little:

Do not fear, for I have redeemed you; I have summoned you by name; you are mine. When you pass through the waters, I will be with you; and when you pass through the rivers, they will not sweep over you. When you walk through the fire, you will not be burned; the flames will not set you ablaze. For I am the Lord your God, the Holy One of Israel, your Savior. (vv 1–3)

When I close my eyes at night, I can rest knowing that He has a plan. I can rest knowing that when He does call me home, I will be ready. Death has no sting for me anymore (1 Corinthians 15:55).

The Lasagna
Multiplication Miracle

BEVERLY LAHOTE SCHWIND

I briskly climbed the crumbling steps of the century-old church building. I carried an armful of blankets as I fought against the wind and snow flurries of the winter day. The man in front of me opened the heavy, weather-worn wooden door, and I walked into the church.

The old building, with its hardwood floors and antique pews, was being used for a different purpose today. My excitement grew as I looked about the room. Some volunteers had arrived earlier and fueled the old stove that sat in the corner of the church. I smelled the wood burning in the woodstove, which worked hard to produce the needed heat, in spite of the cracks in the old building that allowed gusts of wind to enter.

I loved the church building the first time I saw it. The white-siding church had a steeple that was taller than the surrounding trees. The building had been used for a school at one time, and it had outside plumbing and even a well-cared-for cemetery next to it.

On this particular day, our group would be offering clothes, food, and prayers for the people in this poverty-stricken community twenty-five miles from the nearest town.

Clothes hung in rows according to sizes. Shoes and boots lined the wall, standing like soldiers, ready to be moved out. Boxes of food were organized according to family sizes, and frozen turkeys and hams were outside in a trailer.

A table was set up to provide food to the volunteers before their day of distribution work began.

It would be a long day.

Being accepted in this community had been difficult. The folklore and superstitions of many of the residents surrounded everything they did and even how they thought. They were people who didn't attend a church for various reasons. They did not trust people, and accordingly, they were quick to take offense.

During the summer, our small mission team had repaired roofs and insulated some of the weather-beaten homes. The children went with us and helped clean people's yards. The mission of the group was to show love and take Jesus to the streets—not asking them to come to church, just showing His love.

We learned about family feuds that continued. The newer generations didn't even know the reasons for the feuds, but still joined them willingly.

Some of the people desired a Bible study but did not feel comfortable going to the church, so a home group was started.

These people felt more comfortable in the houses of their neighbors than in a church building, so that is where the pastor started.

But we wondered how many would come today—would they accept what we could give them? Would they come to the church that had stood in their community for over a hundred years, and receive food and clothing from a group of people they were unsure of? Would we be good representatives of Christ?

The fifteen volunteers were all ages, and the young children were enthusiastic about the day. A box of stuffed toys was set out, plus a box of games, jump ropes, and balls. The children sorted through the collection, making fun comments. The volunteers would give out the toys if children came.

We'd placed a notice of the event at the one gas station in the area. Word of mouth was still the most effective way to advertise what was happening. The community seemed to have an efficient grapevine. In fact, just one negative word from one of the leaders in the community could nullify our efforts.

We all gathered for prayer two hours before the doors were to open. We had everything organized and ready, so we set a table for our lunch. We figured we'd get our meal out of the way and clean up before any of the townsfolk arrived.

We'd made one large pan of lasagna, which gave us twenty servings. I figured that would be just enough to serve fifteen people, since a few would want second helpings. At least I hoped it would be enough. The wonderful scent of noodles, meat, cheese, and sauce had already aroused our appetites, and I knew from experience how quickly lasagna could disappear!

We had barely filled our plates and begun eating when

there was a knock on the church door. Our first family had arrived to receive what we had to offer.

I greeted them. But instead of focusing on the clothes, shoes, toys, or even the boxes of food, their eyes zeroed in on the fragrant lasagna. Before I could say a word, they were ready to dig in to the pan.

"It looks really good," the young boy commented as he picked up a plate.

I froze. We couldn't tell them the lasagna was not meant for them. If we turned them away from the scant pan of lasagna, it would ruin the ministry we were trying to build.

I looked at what was left in the pan and quickly calculated, sighing with relief. There would be enough.

The church door was now opening continually, two hours early, as the people came. Just like the first family, all of them ignored the clothes, boxes of food, and other items. Instead, they went straight to the food table, where the pan of lasagna seemed to beckon them.

All of us volunteers collectively held our breath. I watched, as did the other workers, as the people filled their plates. Would there be enough?

Three men showed up who were members of the church and went to look at a house in need of repairs. When they returned, they took paper plates and dished up their lasagna.

There was enough.

More and more people came early and automatically headed to the table that had been set up for the fifteen workers. We watched as they piled the lasagna on their plates and then came back for refills. Still, somehow lasagna remained in the pan.

The distribution of the boxes of food began on schedule, but first the people strolled up and down the clothes racks, pulling out different sizes. They talked back and forth and helped each other make the best clothing choices. They picked up clothes for friends who were not there. I could see this was becoming a social event, and the people were enjoying themselves. They asked each other about old friends and about the health of new friends. The children volunteers happily handed out and demonstrated the toys, and picked the right stuffed animal for babies.

The building was warm inside, not because the woodstove was doing its job, but because the room was filled with people and laughter.

The men helped a wheelchair-bound woman enter the room. She had been in a car accident and had lost the use of her legs. I squatted down to look into her eyes and welcome her to the event. She thanked me . . . and then set her wheels toward the pan of lasagna.

All afternoon the people came. The man who'd had a new roof put on by our volunteers had told everyone about the project. He was a person they all seemed to look up to and respect.

We were well received because of the work of love our men had done in the community. Tales of the community were told. We began to understand the people even better and were able to forge fledgling friendships.

At the end of the day, all the boxes of food were gone, and the hams and turkeys had found new homes. Loose hangers dangled on the racks; most of the clothes were taken and a few pairs of shoes still stood, but not one boot was left.

The lasagna pan remained on the table—but it was not empty!

More than sixty people had eaten from the serving for twenty.

Bonnie said, "Does anyone want lasagna to take home?" We all stood amazed. We gave thanks to the Lord. We knew He multiplied the lasagna, just as He had multiplied the bread and the fishes in the Bible.

And there was even some left over.

God provides. Even if He has to work a miracle to do so!

The Battle for Aunt Helen's Soul

Marcia K. Leaser

When the nursing home called and said Aunt Helen was having a bad day, I immediately jumped in my car and went to see what was going on.

Since my aunt and I had just been shopping the day before, I couldn't even imagine what had caused this anxious call. I didn't expect what I found.

As I walked into her room, an ugly feeling disturbed me. I sensed a frightening presence, and the pungent odor of sulfur almost stifled me. I felt an uneasiness I wasn't sure I even wanted to understand.

My first instinct was to run, but knowing God wanted me there, I knelt beside her and softly spoke her name. Her frantic eyes looked into mine and her shaking hands grabbed me.

"I'm dying!" she shrieked.

I didn't know what to say.

"They're coming after me!" she screamed. "They're on fire, they're all dressed in red, and they're coming after me."

Her restless eyes searched mine.

"I'm so afraid! Don't let me die like this," her frantic voice pleaded.

"I'll stay with you tonight," I whispered as I caressed her wrinkled cheek.

The hours passed slowly, and quite often she sat up in bed with frightened eyes that saw something I couldn't see.

"They're here!" she would cry out. "They're going to get me."

By this time I'd figured out what the ugly feeling was. A battle was going on in that tiny room. A fight between Satan and Jesus for Aunt Helen's soul. I could actually smell the conflict.

At ten o'clock that night I knew I needed to ask Aunt Helen an important question. I asked the nurse sitting across the room for a few minutes alone with my aunt. The efficient woman smiled and walked out of the room.

I always felt that my aunt hadn't accepted Jesus as her Savior. She knew who Jesus was and believed He was God's Son, but I'd wanted to talk to her about whether she'd taken the final step to salvation and asked Him into her heart.

I always dismissed the nagging feeling because I felt I had plenty of time to confront her with this. Now I was worried it might be too late.

Her eyes were closed most of the time. But every now and then she'd open them wide and look fearfully into the darkness before her.

"Aunt Helen?" I asked in as calm a voice as I could muster.

She turned and looked directly into my eyes. I knew she was aware of what I was saying.

Breathing a prayer for strength, I whispered, "I have something to ask you."

Her eyes were glued to mine.

"Have you ever asked Jesus into your heart?"

She looked quickly away, and I had my answer.

"I know you love Jesus and always have," I quickly soothed. "But you must accept Him as your Savior by asking Him into your heart."

Her tormented eyes again looked briefly into mine. A sadness filled them that I'd never seen before.

My mother had told me many years before that Aunt Helen had had an abortion when she was a young woman, and I'd always thought she felt unworthy of life because of it. A sixty-eight-year-old sin had kept her from the many blessings our Father in heaven had for her on this earth. That one decision had burdened her through her entire life. Now she was afraid to die because she didn't feel worthy of heaven.

"Aunt Helen," I began softly. "Do you feel you're not going to heaven because of the abortion you had when you were eighteen?"

She lowered her head, and her blue eyes filled with tears.

"God forgave you a long time ago, Aunt Helen," I said. "But you're still harboring shame and guilt. Please forgive yourself and ask Jesus into your heart. Then you'll be assured of your place in heaven."

Several minutes passed and I could feel the battle still raging in the shadowy room. My heart pounded and my nose burned with the stench of Satan.

Suddenly, Aunt Helen grabbed both my hands. She wrapped

her bony fingers tightly around mine and said in an authoritative voice, "Lord Jesus, come into my heart!"

We both heaved a mighty sigh of relief as I gathered her into my arms.

The room was immediately filled with peace. The battle was over, and once again Jesus had been victorious.

The rest of the night I sang and read the Bible to my aunt.

Only once after that did she cry out that they were coming after her. I countered with, "They can't get you, Aunt Helen. You now belong to Jesus."

Still, today, I can see the peace in her eyes as she smiled at me and settled into the pillow.

Death came at 10:10 the next morning. My eyes filled with tears at the loss of my dear aunt. But tears of joy quickly followed because I knew she was safe in the arms of Jesus.

I thanked God that He'd chosen me to talk to Aunt Helen about her salvation. I thanked Him, also, for the lesson I learned in those few tormented hours. I learned that our Savior never gives up on us, that He's fighting for our souls as long as there is breath in our bodies.

Plucked From the Pit

SUSAN E. RAMSDEN

Peggy, don't be such a worrywart! Janie plays around here all the time. It's perfectly safe. Let the girls have a good time together while we have our meeting," said Myrtle, my mother's new friend and business partner.

"I don't know if this is such a good idea, Myrtle. After all, this *is* a construction site. There could be all kinds of hazardous materials and equipment they could get hurt on." Mother grimaced.

A warm summer breeze slipped through the open window, billowing the curtains and beckoning us to run the untamed meadows of childhood.

"I promise I'll be careful. Oh, Mommy, puleeeeze!" I gripped her hand and begged to play with Janie. I had heard the haunting cry of adventure in my spirit.

My poor mother, who was sometimes criticized for being too cautious with her only child, reluctantly decided to let me go, not wanting to appear overly protective or to stifle my attempts to gain some small independence.

Myrtle opened the back door of the mobile home office and shooed her daughter and me out into a strange and exciting new playground.

Cricket songs and a choir of bedding birds in the rustling sycamore converged in summer's carefree song. I was filled with the joyful abandon that only a child at play can fully know. I was four years old. I had a brand-new friend, and I couldn't wait to explore with her the construction site, where our parents produced pre-fab, low-cost homes.

In this shoe-shedding, tree-climbing, tire-swinging season, Janie and I ran through the cemented, chain-link-fenced construction area. When you're four, you can fashion fun out of anything and anywhere. We somersaulted on the front office lawn, practiced our cartwheels, and tap-danced on the wood deck just like budding Shirley Temples.

Trotting, tumbling, yelping, spinning, leaping—we were one with earth and sky and every living thing . . . until adventure called us to a new arena, one that Janie had never before explored.

I still recall running and squealing in delight as I looked over my shoulder to see if my new playmate was gaining on me in our frenetic game of tag.

Suddenly, my joy ended and I was plunged into a deep, dark hole in the cement!

Pain tore at my face and hands, and fear tore at my spirit. My mind reeled as I tried to determine what had just happened. I only knew that moments before, I'd been enjoying a marvelous time, and now I was trapped in a deep pit.

Janie peered over the edge at me and disappeared. She was the only one who knew where I was or what had happened, and now she was gone.

Even more overwhelming than the physical pain was the panic that engulfed me as I realized that I was a captive in this cement cell. I was certain Janie had gone off to explore and that I was now on my own.

I felt completely abandoned—imprisoned and forsaken.

Later in life, when I read the story of Joseph in the Old Testament, I felt a kinship and empathy for him when his brothers threw him into the cistern. I understood how afraid and alone he must have felt.

I spun frantically around and around and cried out. The hole was narrow and the sides were smooth, with no steps or notches for me to use to climb out.

Surely I'm going to die here! I thought.

Childlike, I never reasoned that eventually my parents would realize something was amiss when I didn't return, and would come searching for me.

Hours seemed to pass without any relief, and then, suddenly, inexplicably, I was standing over the abyss, looking down at where I had just been imprisoned.

As I turned and ran toward the mobile home office, Mother ran toward me. She swooped me into her embrace and tried to comfort me and learn exactly what had happened. Little Janie cried right along with me. Not only had she not abandoned me, but she had also alerted Mother to my plight.

After my wounds were treated and bandaged and I had settled down a bit, we went back to view the pit. We discovered that this hole in the cement was designed for a man to stand in and work on the underside of the modular homes without the discomfort of lying on his back. Perhaps it was only six feet deep, but to a tiny child it might as well have been sixty.

The adults were astounded that I had gotten out without help. They inspected the manhole for anything to grasp or use as a foothold. Nothing.

"It's as smooth as a baby's bottom," Janie's dad exclaimed, scratching his head. "How in the world did she get out of there?"

As an adult, recalling that terrifying incident, which is forever imprinted upon my memory, I have often wondered if I really was unaided in my escape, after all. I didn't yet know the Lord, but He knew me! His Word is full of incidences when He sent His angels to aid those in distress. Since there was no earthly explanation for my escaping on my own, I'm convinced that I had a boost from one of God's heavenly helpers.

Now when I'm stuck in a pit of physical or emotional pain, I recall the Lord's compassion shown to that panicky little four-year-old, and I know He always sees me, no matter how deep the chasm I've fallen into. He knows the pain or panic I am experiencing. His Word assures us that His heart is filled with compassion for us when we suffer, and it assures us that when we fall, He will rescue us.

King David recorded in Psalm 103:4 that God "redeems your life from the pit and crowns you with love and compassion."

Just as I rested in Mother's comforting arms that evening long ago, I can now rest knowing that I am forever safe in God's eternal arms of love.

Machine Guns
and Sleeping Ghosts

Peggy Cunningham

The rickety old bus climbed to 14,000 feet above sea level on a dirt road; we were in the Andes Mountains of Bolivia.

As the bus reached the top of the mountain, I marveled at God's creation. It was like being on top of the world.

But then I began to fear for our safety as the old bus began to chug down the mountain rapidly. Glancing out the window, I was looking at the edge of the road with thousand-foot or more drop-offs, no guardrails, and a crazy driver at the wheel. This was the Pan American Highway, but it was much more like a back road cut in the side of the mountain.

When we entered a mountain village, the bus suddenly stopped. I saw Quechua Indian ladies in their native dress selling fruit and bread. They were trying to get our attention by shouting out in Spanish the items they had for sale.

The mountain air was crisp—a welcome relief from the hot and humid climate in the lowlands, where we had been for two weeks—but the dust and thin air had me gasping for breath. In a moment I was gasping for another reason: Suddenly, out of nowhere, uniformed military men with machine guns surrounded the bus!

Two weeks before, our son, Chuck, fifteen, had contracted typhoid fever at the mission school where we worked. We were afraid he was going to die, since we had no way to get him to the city hospital eight hours away. Torrential rains fell all over Bolivia, making it impossible for the mission plane to reach the school. Since many roads and bridges had been washed away, we couldn't reach the city by land either.

A few days later the rains began to let up, but the mission radio couldn't make contact with mission headquarters in the city. Thankfully, we had a ham radio and were able to request help. A plane was finally sent to our aid.

After two weeks of treatment in a city hospital, my son was released and we were returning to the school in a bus that looked a hundred years old. My son, sitting next to me, was still weak and looking frail after losing nearly thirty pounds.

I was concerned the trip would cause him to relapse if all didn't go well. The conditions of the roads and the buses made me wonder if we could ever travel in Bolivia without encountering problems. Often there were landslides and roadblocks, and more often than not, mechanical problems with the buses.

We were traveling in a small, dilapidated bus much like a school bus; people were carrying their chickens and pigs to sell in the marketplace, and the driver seemed to be in a race with other bus drivers to see who could go the fastest over dangerous roads. Needless to say, all of this was not exactly helpful for a teenage passenger recovering from a life-threatening disease.

And now we faced another problem: the military was detaining the bus to search for drugs and check our IDs.

It was our first year in Bolivia and everything was still new and strange to us. This trip was the first time I had traveled without my whole family by my side—my husband and daughter were waiting for us back at the mission school. So I was feeling anything but calm when the armed military soldiers entered the bus.

My son was relaxed beside me, but he didn't realize we didn't have any form of identification with us. Our passports were in the capital city of La Paz to process our permanent visas, and we were left without anything else to identify us. Normally, people with no proof of permission to be in the country were immediately arrested and taken to the nearest prison, especially foreigners.

Prison in an underdeveloped country is not a place anyone wants to experience; just a few weeks before, I had visited one of them. I went with a group of missionary ladies to visit a young American lady who'd been arrested as she was leaving the country with cocaine in her possession.

The prison trip was shocking for me, a new missionary. In the prison, the smells were horrific and the living conditions appalling. Her cell had only a concrete floor with no bathroom or bed, and she had nothing but the clothes on her back. Her only meals were what people from the outside brought to her.

The lady had no one to help her, so a ministry began as we took food, clothes, and God's Word to her each day, meeting her needs in every way we could. She came to know the Lord and began witnessing to the other prisoners, a ministry within a ministry. Eventually, she was extradited to the United States and left Bolivia a new creation in Christ.

That prison scene was now on my mind. What would happen when they discovered we had no identification to show them? Would they take us to prison?

I told my son the problem we faced and announced that the only thing we could do was pray. I said, "Put your head down, close your eyes, and pretend you are sleeping. Don't open your eyes unless they insist. We are going to pray they don't see us."

My son looked at me as though I had lost my mind, but I assured him God would take care of us.

I glanced down the aisle once more and saw at least ten soldiers with their machine guns. That didn't give me much peace in my heart. I prayed that God would put a hedge around us and that we would be overlooked.

Even as I prayed, I knew I was asking the impossible. How could they miss two tall blondes with white skin in a bus filled with short people who had black hair and dark skin?

One by one people on the bus were checked—their luggage, their bodies, and their possessions. We could hear the baggage being taken out of the compartment under the bus. Every inch of the bus was being searched.

We kept our heads down and our eyes shut.

We were in the middle of the bus and, as they came down the aisle, I could hear their questions. They spoke with authority; it was intimidating to a foreigner in a strange land.

They came closer. The people sitting in front of us were asked to step into the aisle and were searched. The baggage over our heads was taken down, searched, and returned to the compartment.

My heart was racing and I couldn't tell if my son was breathing, he was so quiet.

I opened one eye just enough to glimpse the soldier's boots moving to the seat behind us. We kept our composure and kept our eyes shut. They were moving past us.

The soldier's machine gun bumped my head as he passed, but he didn't ask us to step out. Didn't he know he had hit my head with his machine gun? Was I just a sleeping ghost to him?

It was as though we were frozen in time; we were like statues with our eyes shut until they passed. And even then we didn't move.

Hours seemed to pass until they reached the back of the bus, finished their search, walked back through the bus, and then exited out the front doors.

"Are you okay?" I whispered to my son. "Stay still until the bus leaves."

In moments, the engine roared, the bus jerked, and we were on our way.

What had just happened?

We thanked God for answered prayer. It was as though we were two ghosts, invisible in those two seats in the bus. Had God sent His angels to encompass us? Had He made us invisible? Were the soldiers blinded to our existence?

We only knew He had intervened in a supernatural way. He had protected us from any harm and perhaps even rescued us from the pit of a Bolivian prison—where my son could never have survived if we had been detained for any length of time. It was a miraculous rescue from unknown dangers.

When our bus finally turned off the bumpy road into the mission school, we couldn't wait to exit that bus and tell of God's miraculous protection.

Does God still do miracles today? Does He do things that seem impossible to us but possible with Him? Does He answer our prayers?

You bet He does.

Psalm 4:8 says, "In peace I will lie down and sleep, for you alone, Lord, make me dwell in safety."

That verse came to me that day as my son and I pretended to sleep. I felt peace knowing that He alone keeps us safe—sleeping or awake, with or without machine guns passing by our heads, and even while pretending to sleep.

Help Wanted:
Divine Domestic

SANDI BANKS

I f there had been an organization called Moms in Distress, I'd have surely been its poster child that spring day in 1978. My postpartum world had begun unraveling ten days earlier, as I shuffled through the door of our little base house in Woodbridge, England—fresh from the hospital, with a screaming newborn, her energetic fifteen-month-old sister, and a U.S. Air Force pilot husband who would soon don his flight suit, fling his large duffel bag into our 1949 Ford Poplar, and wave good-bye as he left on a six-week military deployment. Family and friends were an ocean away. I felt desperately alone.

I'm cheerful by nature, so this was uncharted territory for me: the waves of despair, the heaviness of heart, and the unyielding weight of responsibility.

If I can just make it through this one chore, things will get better, I kept reasoning.

But for every task I completed, three more surfaced. I sank slowly into a recliner that had seen better days and tried to soothe a disgruntled infant and satisfy a needy toddler. Then I surveyed my surroundings and sighed.

Every room looked as if a tsunami had hit. Demands on my time and energy piled up almost as fast as the dirty cloth diapers in the pail. Needs. Everywhere, needs! Needs of my newborn daughter, whose flailing arms and shrill, round-the-clock cries baffled doctors and unnerved me. Needs of my lively fifteen-month-old, who wandered from room to room, knocking over toy boxes, dumping out hampers, and persistently petitioning Mommy to "weed me a 'tory." Needs, relentless needs, of daily life—the cooking, the cleaning, the toppling mountain of laundry calling my name.

Not just outwardly, but inwardly, a gnawing sense of hope-lessness prevailed as I became physically spent, trying to recover from a difficult delivery and sleepless nights; emotionally drained, missing the moral support of husband, family, and friends; and mentally overwhelmed, spiraling downward without anyone to catch me.

Finally, I just lost it. Loud sobs ushered in a sense of utter despair.

"I give up!" I cried. "Somebody please help me! I can't do this!"

Within moments, over the din of a wailing newborn and babbling toddler, I heard a knock at the door.

"Umm, who's there?" I managed to halfheartedly coax the words out of my mouth, swiping at tears with the back of my hand.

I couldn't imagine who it would be, since surely no one

this side of the Atlantic would be paying me a visit. Nor could I imagine anyone seeing my house or me looking like this—the girls and I were far from hostess mode. In fact, I wished that whoever it was would just go away. Reluctantly, I navigated through the sea of debris.

Before I could reach the door to unlatch it, it sprung open. A round, rosy-cheeked woman with speckles of gray in her hair and sunshine in her smile invited herself in, latching the door behind her.

"Halloo! Top o' the mornin'!" she chirped, removing her woolly green sweater and multicolored crocheted scarf, carefully draping them over the chair by the door. She put on the teakettle and made herself quite at home, as if we were longtime girlfriends and I was expecting her visit.

I don't recall her exact words, but I do remember the sense of relief I felt when she insisted that I sit and rock the baby, who instantly quieted down and drifted into a blissful sleep— a rare treat for both mother and child.

Before I could gather my wits or utter a word, this stranger started in to work, swiftly and effortlessly, humming as she went.

Her first order of business was to lovingly sweep my sleepy toddler into her arms, kiss her on the cheek, and gently lay her down for a much-needed morning nap. My mother heart melted as my newborn baby snuggled peacefully in my arms, her colicky screams replaced by contented sighs.

Another transformation was taking place around us—at lightning speed. I watched in awe as the mystery woman swiftly tackled the sink full of dishes, the laundry, the sheets, the rugs, the floors—washing, polishing, sweeping, mopping, and even pulling freshly baked meals from the oven. How could a stranger possibly know where everything was, and where everything went—cleaning supplies, pots and pans, clothes, toys—as comfortably as if she lived here herself?

From my little corner of the world, a comfy wooden rocking chair, I watched this amazing metamorphosis unfold.

How surreal! Never could I have imagined such a scene—a stranger taking over my home, and I, totally at peace about it. I don't remember even questioning who she was, where she had come from, or why she was doing this. I just remember an extraordinary calm cascading over me, refreshing and renewing me, as I witnessed my crumbling world returning to order.

In no time at all, I had been given the gift of a sparkling home, sleeping children, scrumptious meals, and peace— "peace that surpasses all understanding."

Then she was gone, as suddenly as she had come.

"Wait! Please!" I called as she closed the door behind her.

Seconds later I stood on the sidewalk, looking up and down the street. But she was nowhere in sight. I turned to three people who were standing by my house, chatting.

"Which way did she go?"

"Who?"

"The woman who just came out my door!"

They looked at each other, then back at me, and shrugged. They had been there the whole time, yet not one of them had seen anyone enter or leave my house.

Wow. I walked back into my pristine, orderly home, peeked in on my precious babies all snug in their cribs, and marveled, trying to process what had just happened. It would be a while before I could share this story with anyone, or acknowledge what I ultimately came to believe.

God heard my cry and sent an angel to revive my spirit, meet my needs, and above all, to bring Him glory. For they were needs that no one knew about but me. It was a major turning point—not only in my practical need of the moment, but in my spiritual need of a lifetime. I began to realize and confess how far I had drifted from the Lord, not by blatant rebellion, but by busyness and worldly distractions. I could not imagine God loving me that much, listening, caring, providing, in such a dramatic way. It was the first step in my journey back to God's heart.

Who would have thought that a perky woman in a green sweater could play such a critical role in bringing me back to the Lord? It all remains a great mystery. It's unexplainable apart from God's grace and His supernatural response to the plight of a young Mom in Distress and her desperate plea for help.

God on the Phone

DEBI DOWNS

Tears flowed down my cheeks, collecting on the thin pages of the open Bible on my lap. Each drop ushered in another wave of sadness.

Looking down, I felt one puddle that had formed on the Bible represented my marriage—dead through a divorce, and buried under the water. In another pool, I saw the faces of my mother and brother, who had recently died within three months of each other. Each tear that continued to splash represented the loss of something—my home, a job, and my children moving away. I sobbed as if the best parts of life were gone forever.

"God, do you even know I'm here?" I prayed. "Why don't you answer me when I call your name? Do you see me? God, do you care? You left me to face this life all alone and . . . I do not understand your ways, Lord!"

I glanced at the clock on the wall. Forty-three minutes wasted on some kind of a spiritual meltdown, a "poor pitiful, God-love-ya, Debi," moment when in less than an hour I needed to be at work.

While I wiped tears with the sleeve of my robe, I snuffed all emotion. Gradually, I put on the cheery disposition I needed for my job and was out the door.

My company is in the business of collecting delinquent auto, boat, and trailer payments. I slid into my chair and said hello to my co-worker Brittany and logged on to the computer that connected to the company's phone router. My job was to secure payments over the phone or to leave a message for the person to return my call.

I was two hours into my work when a call came through. Instantly, the computer screen displayed the caller's name and address.

"This is Debi. How may I help you?"

Miss Smith wanted to make a car payment. Her voice sounded gentle and high. A thick, drawn-out Georgia drawl confirmed her Southern roots.

I took the payment information, thanked her, and then waited for her response.

There was a long silence.

"Miss—Debi? Is that your name? Miss Debi?"

I could not help but smile as I answered. "Yes, ma'am, that is my name."

"Well . . . I feel like I can't hang up just yet."

After another hesitation, Miss Smith's voice deepened and the accent was less prominent. She spoke with clear authority as if to be sure I understood every word.

"Miss Debi, God wants me to tell you . . . He sees your tears. He hears you when you cry. He knows your prayers.

223

Do not be afraid. He'll be with you every minute of every day. His ways are unknown to you, but trust in Him. You are never alone. He has not forgotten nor forsaken you. He'll be with you always."

I waited, my heart beating faster.

Please tell me there is more—what else does God want me to know?

I listened for more, but that was all. I could not speak. My hands trembled and I felt a warmth envelop me as tears of unbridled happiness and unrestrained joy slid down my face. I sat in amazement and awe understanding . . .

God just called me on the phone!

He answered every question I had that morning, exactly as I had taken them before Him. He reaffirmed a love for me that only my God knew I needed and sent that message in words I knew had come from Him alone.

That reassurance now flowed through the phone lines; Miss Smith was His vessel.

I was startled by the soft touch of a hand on my shoulder. In front of me a Kleenex appeared as Brittany rolled her chair next to mine.

"Hey, don't cry. I know how you feel," she whispered. "Mean calls like that come in all the time. Just forget about it."

I just shook my head as she turned back to answer her next call.

"Miss Debi? Miss Debi?"

The sound of her voice focused my attention.

"Ummm . . ." was all I could say.

"I'm sorry to be troubling you! You need to get back to work."

"No, Miss Smith, you have not troubled me at all, not at all."

I searched for the right words. How could I express my gratitude to a stranger who willingly opened her spirit and gave our heavenly Father complete access?

"You've given me more peace than you'll ever know. Thank you for my message. Thank you."

I had heard God's voice before. However, that morning, the sorrow from all my loss was so alarmingly disruptive, I could not hear Him. The wall I built around my spirit blocked His presence. I did not know He had been sitting patiently, lovingly beside me all along to provide guidance, strength, and comfort.

He had never left my side. And through Miss Smith, he called me to let me know.

Trial by Fire

SUSAN A. J. LYTTEK

Shortly after I came to faith in Christ, all hell broke loose. My husband, Gary, and I dismissed the first noises and bangs. Perhaps our neighbors were fighting again. They did that often enough and we could hear it through our shared wall. Or maybe the cats knocked something over while they were playing. Surely logic could explain things falling and breaking.

I hoped it could. Though I rejoiced in my new relationship with Jesus, I could not explain the feeling of darkness that pressed in on me.

Then one night, Gary and I were in our room praying, both cats nestled at the foot of the bed, when we heard a loud crash.

We headed downstairs and saw a framed picture on the

floor in the center of the living room. No way—no natural way—existed for it to have made it to that position.

I began to shake and sob. "Let me go! Let me go!"

Gary wrapped his arms around me. I was so terrified I could barely feel his embrace. The darkness seemed to be everywhere and the night more intense. After he went to bed, I grabbed my Bible like a lifeline and read until morning. In the light, I finally fell asleep.

When I went to work the next evening, I told my boss—who had witnessed to me and prayed for me since I had begun working with him—what had been happening.

"Sounds like spiritual warfare," John said.

"But why now? Why me?"

"From what I've read, things like ghosts and poltergeists are probably demons. Have you had involvement with them in the past?"

"Probably," I admitted. "But that was years ago. I gave it all up after I got scared at a cult meeting when I was sixteen."

"Gave all what up?" he persisted as we set the tables for that night's banquet.

I wiped the next table as I thought of a way to answer him. The past wasn't simple.

"I was really into astrology for a few years. I used to chart the signs and aspects for people I wanted to be my friends. It helped me get noticed and feel powerful. So I looked further into the occult, read palms and such."

John must have heard the unfinished sound at the end of my sentence. "And . . . ?"

"And I had a spirit guide that showed me futures."

The former bike-gang member turned chef nodded knowingly. "That would do it."

"But I stopped communicating with it when I gave up the occult!"

"Maybe. But without God to fill you, I bet it hung around." Then he lowered his voice. "Or worse, came back with others like in Luke 11:26."

That made me curious to see what the Bible said on the matter but also hesitant to read it and find out why I had the chills. Then he cleared his throat and I looked up. The coordinators for the night's activities had arrived. "You go start the coffee. We'll talk later. And pray."

The night, as most times when the club hosted a banquet, passed in a blur of faces and activity. The last of the guests left shortly after 1:00 a.m., and the clock by the front offices chimed 2:00 before we finished cleaning up.

As he did whenever we worked into the wee hours, John pulled the staff over to the table near the coffee machine to pray for our safe journey home. "Lord, watch over these dear ladies as they return to their husbands tonight. May they drive safely and stay alert. We praise you again for Susan's new faith. And, Jesus, we ask you for wisdom for her and Gary on how to overcome the attacks she is experiencing."

He went on to pray for the other waitress about some of her personal needs, and for the busboy, who worried about his next science exam. Then he squeezed our hands farewell and escorted us out to our cars.

Snow had dusted the vehicles while we worked, but the roads were dry. I got in the car and turned the engine on, hoping my Renault would warm up faster than usual. Cranking the tunes up to keep me awake, I headed south on Highway 23, back to the base housing and my sleeping husband.

The rest of the night passed uneventfully. My former guide appeared to be sleeping. But the following day came early, since I had to be in class at 9:00. Only copious amounts of coffee and diet cola kept me awake and alert through the seven hours of lectures. Around 4:00 p.m., I returned home in time to take a short nap before heading back to the country club. Gary hadn't yet returned from golfing with his friend Karl.

I curled up on the couch with our cat Chat-Chat. As I started to nod off, I heard noises from the extra room upstairs—the one whose door was always shut and where we kept the weight set. My heart began to race, and fear threatened to overwhelm me. Carrying the cat so I wouldn't be alone, I raced upstairs, grabbed my work uniform out of the bedroom, then deposited the cat back downstairs by a fresh bowl of kibble and headed to the car.

When I arrived at work, John was at the back door carrying in the food for that night's dinner. Surprised to see me an hour early, he guessed what was wrong.

"You can't continue like this, Susan."

"I know," I moaned.

I helped him carry in a couple of boxes before he spoke again. "I hope you don't mind, but I told Don about what's been happening with you."

I shook my head. I didn't mind. Gary and I had attended Don's house church a couple of times and liked the matter-of-fact way he approached faith. If I had been thinking logically, I would have asked for his opinion.

"He said you probably have possessions associated with your old days. Things you haven't purged yet that your unwanted visitor feels tied to."

"Okay. How do I know what those things are?"

"Think about it. Pray about it. Ask God to show you what reminds you most of your time with the occult."

Fortunately for me, the country club had only its regular member dinner that night, and I was home by ten. I found Gary and told him what John had said.

"I'd guess your heavy metal and druggie albums might remind you of those days. You don't listen to most of them anymore. I don't even know why you have them."

He had a good point.

"Let's get them out of the house then!" I said.

We found one of our old moving boxes and loaded my old records into it. Then we set it on the porch and locked the door.

I slept well that night.

The next day was Sunday. We planned to go to Don's house church that afternoon for worship. We got there a bit early to talk. He asked me question after question about my early teen years and what I did.

"I think Gary was right, that you need to get rid of a lot of your old music. Music has powerful effects on the soul. But you wrote and kept a journal. You said the guide told you to write down certain messages. I think we should go through that."

I hadn't unpacked most of my journals and stories since Gary and I had married. When Don arranged for Gary and me, and John and his wife, Laura, to come to his house the following Sunday for lunch and a memory purge, I wasn't sure what to expect. However, I did agree to bring the boxes.

The six of us enjoyed an excellent lunch. Then we started going through my journals. We hadn't read much before John opened a page, obviously in my handwriting. It described me walking across a narrow bridge, with demons clawing at my feet and legs. I was trying to get to the beautiful angel with the evil eyes on the other side, but an invisible someone kept pushing me back.

"I don't remember writing that," I told them. "How spooky."

"Definitely," agreed John. "But also encouraging."

"How?"

"Who do you think kept you from getting across that bridge? I'd wager God had His hand on you even then. Who do you think helped you see beyond Satan's beauty to the evil in his eyes?"

With everyone's help, in less than an hour we had a huge pile of paper—journal pages to burn.

"This should keep us warm for a while."

Don led us to his large backyard that faced the woods. He dumped the papers into his burn barrel. He handed me a pack of matches.

"Susan, will you do the honors?"

I thought I would feel sad seeing so many years of writing and so much effort go up in smoke, but instead relief filled me. I laughed for the first time since Jesus had called me His own.

I was free.

A Wing and a Prayer

RUTH BISKUPSKI, as told to
NANCY HAGERMAN

Dazed, battered, and covered in blood, I was standing at the top of the embankment.

How did I get here? I asked myself. To this day I don't remember climbing that hill.

The morning had begun with so much excitement. I was sixteen and the night before had purchased my first car. It was an ancient Toyota, primer gray, and cost $200. It had obviously seen better days, but it was brand-new to me, had black leather seat covers, and was drivable.

Dad had his doubts about it because it was so old, but I won him over. I loved it and it was mine.

I hurried to get it insured and licensed that morning so I could drive to my boyfriend's house. I couldn't wait to get my car all fixed up, and he'd promised to put in a set of new speakers.

On my way back out, Mom did her thing.

"Be careful, honey. I'll be praying for you."

Why did she always do that?

I *was* careful. I'd never been in a wreck. Why did I need all that extra prayer? I didn't need her telling me to be careful. I was a good driver. My guardian angels didn't have all that much to do.

My boyfriend, Bob, lived in Colbran, a small town up the mountain, about thirty-five miles from my home in Grand Junction. It was a beautiful drive. I wound through a canyon of towering red rock on either side of the road and then up the mountain by meadows of green grass and wild flowers.

As the road climbed, clumps of aspen and spruce trees began to appear. The road hugged the mountain and sometimes steep drop-offs were on one side or the other. I was used to mountains, though, and I loved the drive. It was so peaceful.

When I arrived, Bob and his brother dutifully admired the car and installed the new speakers. They were great! We listened to music for a while before Bob had to go to work. I was going to follow him down the mountain, but his brother begged me to stay. He and his friends wanted a ride to Grand Junction but were watching a video and asked if I'd wait until it was over.

I said good-bye to Bob and settled in to watch the rest of the movie. As soon as it was over and I stood to leave, the other kids changed their minds and decided they would rather stay. I was miffed, but it was a decision that probably saved their lives. Unbeknownst to me, Mom's prayers were making a difference.

As I drove away, it began to rain heavily. I could have stayed at Bob's house, but I'd been gone quite a while and knew my parents would worry, so I set off anyway. I followed one car for a while, but it was going faster than I wanted to go, so I slowed down. There was hardly anyone on the road.

My car was pulling slightly to the right, but I attributed it to the rain and the slick roads. I didn't think much of it until I heard a *clunk,* and the car swerved abruptly. I fought to gain control.

Being alone and not knowing what else to do, I remained in the car and kept driving.

Clunk!

The car went completely out of control, careened across the road, and went over the embankment. I have no idea how many times it rolled. I only remember seeing sky, grass, sky, grass . . . over and over again. I closed my eyes.

When the car finally stopped, I was hanging upside down from my seat belt. I'd been sure I was going to die, but I slowly opened my eyes. The car was resting upside down in a stream, and water was seeping in. The roof below me was already covered with water.

The gasoline smell was quite strong and I knew I had to get out soon. I looked at my options. The roof was crushed into the rear window, eliminating it. Most of the back seat actually lay on the roof. Where the rear side windows had been there was only twisted metal. Anyone riding in that backseat would have been killed.

I was certainly not going to get out that way. Likewise, the front passenger window frame was crushed, while the hood of the car was smashed into the windshield and blocked any escape from there.

The gasoline fumes were much stronger now, and I worried about fire. I knew I had to help myself—I was sure no one had seen me go off the road. I wriggled out of my seat belt and fell headfirst.

Finally, I got a look at the driver's side window.

The frame was crushed into a V shape, but there was a very small section I might be able to squirm through. Surprisingly, the glass in that V shape was unbroken. How would I break it?

"Lord, help me," I prayed as I took a deep breath and punched the window.

It broke.

I put my head and shoulders through the hole and then became stuck.

I struggled until I was ready to give up and then prayed, *Lord, help me. I can't do this!*

Instantly, I felt strong hands grab hold of mine and pull, while another set of hands pushed me from behind. I popped through that window like a cork. I was thankful that rescuers had arrived, but when I looked around there was no one there.

I was bruised and sore and dreaded climbing up the steep incline above the stream, yet suddenly I found myself at the top with no memory of how I got there.

Just as suddenly, a car appeared. The driver was a nurse and wrapped me in blankets. Her son was a brand-new driver, so while his mother waited with me, he was able to go to town for help.

The rescue squad was all volunteers. When a call for help came in, it usually took about an hour to get everyone together to respond. That night they just happened to be having a meeting and were on the scene within ten minutes.

I was covered with blood, but as the EMTs worked at cleaning me up on the way to the hospital, they found no cuts. The car had been full of flying glass and I had put my hand through a window, but my skin was unbroken.

No one even knew where the blood came from. The only injury on me was a bump on the head I got when I fell after unlatching the seat belt. I was released to my parents' care the same day, shaken but in one piece.

When Dad went to see about towing the car, he couldn't find it. Both he and the tow truck driver looked for a long time before they finally discovered it, upside down and half buried in the stream. It was so well camouflaged by huge cottonwoods that it was invisible from the road. Had I not gotten out, I might not have been found before something serious occurred.

The accident happened when the rear axle had broken off close to the right tire. We found the wheel, still connected to the broken axle, by the side of the road.

I puzzled a long time over my experience before I talked about it with anyone. If I was alone down there, who had gotten me out of the car?

The conclusion I've come to is that my guardian angels were at work. I believe they pulled me out of the car, healed my wounds, and then carried me up the hill to the road.

I believe that I was never alone before or after the wreck. Jesus was watching out for me all the time, whether I thought I needed Him or not.

Today I have children of my own, but whenever I leave Mom's house, she repeats, "Be careful, honey. I'm praying for you."

It doesn't bother me now. In fact, I say the same thing to my own kids. What's more, I know that Jesus and His angels will guard them, even when I can't.

The Knocks, the Books, and the Wardrobe

James Stuart Bell

We were speeding dizzily along the lanes of the Irish countryside, with its cozy thatched cottages dotting the landscape and its forty shades of green. I had recently asked Margaret, a beautiful, raven-haired, emerald-eyed "colleen" from Ireland to marry me. Now was "meet the parents" time. We had stepped off the plane in Dublin an hour before. My heart was pounding with trepidation, my body tired from international jet lag.

Her brother was driving and my soon-to-be spouse asked an innocent question: "How are Mom and Dad?" With his lilting Dublin accent, he intoned, "Ach, they're in fightin' form." She had warned me about her passionate Irish family, who loved and fought with equal measure. And I was supposed to help convert them with my testimony of God's gentle love.

When I arrived, I wasn't prepared for the additional supernatural dimension of the fighting that was taking place under their roof. I felt like I needed to start with a long afternoon nap in order to be fresh and make a good first impression. I crept under a soft down comforter and immediately was in dreamland—until the loud knock at the door. I figured Margaret's parents wanted to make sure I was comfortable, so I got up and opened the door. No one was there. *Not to worry,* I told myself, *I'm disoriented from the jet lag and travel noise.*

But the knocks continued to sound. And each time I called out or got up, no visible soul was present. I felt oppressed and even more fatigued. When Margaret popped her head in, I told her about the noise. She gave me the I-told-you-so look and went off to her own room down the hall, telling me to just sleep through the night and get up early and refreshed the next morning. Great plan—except for the event that was soon to occur.

I had finally fallen into a deep sleep when it happened. About 2:00 a.m. I heard what sounded like a nuclear bomb. My adrenalin soared as I flipped on the light. There, next to my bed, was the eight-foot by four-foot solid oak wardrobe that had been upright, now facedown, with the unfinished wood of the back producing a tabletop effect.

Margaret and her mother were fast on the scene. They both exclaimed in unison, "You poor thing" and, after realizing I was in one piece, we began to examine the wardrobe. The small legs from the foundation were solid as a rock. My future mother-in-law may have wondered what kind of preacher (that's what she thought I was) had entered her home and what ill omens I might have brought with me. But she didn't betray anything negative, and we used the facedown wardrobe as a table for tea and biscuits.

Later, I told Margaret that somebody didn't like me being there, but it wasn't her mom. She suggested we go two doors down to her room and pray against the spiritual forces creating the poltergeists. She said she sensed a word from the Lord that there were evil spirits all around out to attack us, but we need not fear because of His protecting presence. "Oh, and by the way, my aunt read tea leaves and palms in this very room, and my other brother did psychedelic drugs and has some bad books in the middle room," she shared.

I quietly entered Margaret's brother's room and found that his reading tastes were similar to mine—before I became a Christian. Books on paranormal activity, Eastern religions, and occult philosophy abounded. He had long ago left home and the books were gathering dust. Margaret said we should burn them the next morning to purge the house for the sake of her parents. "And for me too. I've got to survive the rest of my stay," I said. We then prayed again and bound all evil spirits, casting them out in the name of Jesus.

The next morning we gathered up the books, snuck out the side door, and created a small conflagration in the field behind the house. I figured if I got caught, I'd be packing my bag back to the States. Or maybe they would thank us for a fall cleaning?

The rest of that stay was peaceful and I slept like a rock, the crisp autumn country air with smells of peat smoke coming through my window at night. My future mother-in-law's delicious breakfasts of bacon, eggs, white and red pudding, fried bread, mushrooms, tomatoes, and Harry Hogg's plump sausages were there to fatten up the "beanpole," as I was secretly called. Refusing a second helping was not allowed, and no one crossed Mom and lived a pleasant life afterward. She couldn't quite figure me out, and later called me a Lutheran preacher because no one had ever seen a Lutheran in her Irish country village before. But as she lay on her deathbed in the hospital, she said I had the face of an angel. Though angel I am not, she may have seen a faint image of Christ within me, as I have seen in others who have modeled Him.

At times, God calls us to do a spiritual housecleaning before He begins new and powerful works in our lives. That housecleaning may be in our souls, our houses, or the environments in which we live and move and have our being.

The Lord was able to establish His presence in my wife's Irish home and bring the adversarial strongholds under control, and both her parents and some siblings made commitments to Christ over the years. We had to continue praying and taking authority, even when later we were not present, in order to prevent, as it states in Luke 11:24–26, the unclean spirits, after leaving that house, from returning and bringing seven more unclean spirits to make their abode there.

We continue to have a spiritual adversary who is out to accuse and deceive if we wish to do the work of Christ; very rarely, that adversary displays his presence to us. But we need not fear because Christ has given us all power and authority over those spirits, in His mighty name.

About the Contributors

Sandi Banks lives in Texas and is the author of *Anchors of Hope*. She works for Summit Ministries and enjoys traveling and ministering in various countries.

James Stuart Bell is the compiler of this volume and numerous other volumes of inspirational short stories, including A CUP OF COMFORT and the EXTRAORDINARY ANSWERS TO PRAYER series.

Ruth Biskupski calls Grand Junction, Colorado, home.

Connie Brown is married to a kind husband and is a mother of four and a grandmother of five. Her writing has appeared in Christian and local publications.

Sally Burbank practices internal medicine as a career. She spends her free time nurturing two teens, tending a large country garden, teaching Sunday school, reading, and sweating at the YMCA.

Billy Burch is a pastor at Christ Community Church. He received his B.S. at Liberty University and an M.Div. and M.A. at Trinity Evangelical Divinity School.

Kristin H. Carden is a Christian counselor at her private practice in South Carolina. Her heart is for people to experience true freedom from fear and inner healing through Jesus Christ.

Laura Chevalier lives in Colorado and coordinates programs for international students and short-term mission teams. She also enjoys hiking, biking, and writing (www.hope-on-the-journey.blogspot.com).

Charles D. Cochran has a ministry that spans twenty-five years—acting, writing, and directing Christmas/Easter musical dramas including an adaptation of Max Lucado's *An Angel's Story*. He resides in Denver with his wife, Sharon.

Liz Collard is a Christ follower, wife, and mother from Orlando. Author of the BUILDING A GODLY MARRIAGE series, her heart's desire is to see families serving and glorifying God together.

Craig Cornelius is an avid outdoorsman who will hunt and fish any chance he gets. He is married and has three kids and two dogs. He lives in Chester County, Pennsylvania.

Fran Courtney-Smith lived in Africa from the time her British missionary parents went there in 1947. Fran served as a career missionary in Africa, delivering over four thousand babies there. Retired, she lives in Arcadia, California.

Kat Crawford is the author of *Capsules of Hope: Survival Guide for Caregivers.* She is published in fifteen compilations and numerous magazines. Read about her journey on www. caringbridge.org/visit/kat2009 or http://lionheartedkat.com.

Peggy Cunningham and her husband have been missionaries in Bolivia since 1981. She has written thirteen children's books and contributes to *The Voice of Grace and Truth* and *Devo Kids.*

Sally Edwards Danley began her writing career in the 1980s and is a leader in the Heart of America Christian Writers Network. See her Facebook page and her website: www.sallysdoor.vpweb.com.

Debi Downs is from Joplin, Missouri. At her music studio, A Joyful Noise, she teaches talented piano, violin, and Kindermusik students.

Loretta J. Eidson is enrolled in Jerry Jenkins' Christian Writer's Guild Journeyman course and has had short stories published in several anthologies.

Beatrice Fishback, along with her husband, Jim, is coauthor of *Defending the Military Marriage* and *Defending the Military Family.* She is also the author of *Loving Your Military Man.*

Connie Green grew up in southwest Kansas, graduated from Kansas University, and worked at Hallmark Cards before marrying Tim Green and becoming a homemaker and mother of three. She passed away in 2006 from cancer.

Nancy Hagerman is a writer and speaker from western Colorado. She is the author of *In the Pit: A Testimony of God's Faithfulness to a Bipolar Christian.*

Charles Earl Harrel served as a pastor for thirty years. He has over three hundred fifty published works. His stories and devotionals have appeared in various magazines, including twenty-four book compilations.

Bob Haslam has served as a pastor, missionary, and magazine and book editor. He served as an executive with World Relief, the international relief arm of the National Association of Evangelicals.

Anneliese Jawinski loves to help anyone in need to achieve spiritual and physical well-being. She is also an organic gardener and a daily pole walker.

Linda Jett lives in Newberg, Oregon, where she gives massages, participates in Celebrate Recovery, and joins her husband of thirty-two years in their church's drama ministry.

Pat Stockett Johnston is a multi-published author of devotionals, books, and articles. She lives in Temple City, California.

Suzan Klassen is published in *101 Facets of Faith* and *Focus on Your Child*. However, her only true claim to fame is that God put her name in His Book of Life.

Marcia K. Leaser has more than nine hundred pieces published, including a children's book, *Frizzeldee's Catastrophe,* and a woman's devotional, *Every Step of the Way.*

Susan A. J. Lyttek, award-winning writer, wife to Gary, and homeschool mother of two teenage boys, writes early mornings in the shadow of our nation's capital.

Robert A. McCaughan, after retiring from the Air Force, became a church pastoral counselor. Later he served as the Chairperson of the Counseling Department at Luther Rice Seminary.

Mike McKown went through Aviation Cadet Training with Robert McCaughan. Both were awarded their wings as navigators and commissioned as second lieutenants at the same time. He is a retired Vietnam veteran.

David Milotta is a retired pastor living in Hawaii. Married with two adult children, he loves Great Danes, windsurfing, and stand-up paddle surfing. He is the author of *Faithbuildings: Partnering with God for Miracles.*

Joe Murphy is the pastor of St. Aidan's Anglican Church in Oswego, Illinois, and a professor who teaches at various colleges and seminaries.

Jane Owen is a freelance writer who enjoys retirement in the woods of West Virginia. She and her husband, Ron, were missionaries in Haiti for almost three years.

Donald E. Phillips is a former chaplain, professor, pastor, and author of four internationally recognized academic books and shorter writings on prayer, God's will, grief recovery, and other topics.

Connie K. Pombo is a "retired" author, speaker, and freelance writer who lives in Cuenca, Ecuador. She has contributed to several story anthologies and can be reached at www.conniepombo.com.

Susan E. Ramsden, a writer and speaker, enjoys encouraging others with her spiritual poetry and devotionals. She has been published in several anthologies.

Angie Reedy delights in finding evidence of God's extraordinary greatness in the ordinary happenings of life. She lives in central Illinois with her husband and three children.

Jonathan Reiff, a semi-retired tax lawyer in Oklahoma, received his Army commission through ROTC at Harvard. He lives with his wife, Roz, two daughters, and five grandchildren in Edmond, Oklahoma.

Linda W. Rooks is the author of *Broken Heart on Hold* and has written short pieces for various anthologies.

Tina Samples lives with her husband and two boys in Colorado and attends Grace River Church. She is a worship leader, speaker, teacher, and author. You can find her at www.tina-samples.com.

Beverly LaHote Schwind is the author of four books and writes a newspaper column, *Patches of Life*. She volunteers at the Care Center and teaches in a jail and rehabilitation center. She and her husband are retired and live in Tennessee.

Cheryl Secomb likes to write fiction and has had four short stories published and one devotional pending publication. She is a member of Oregon Christian Writers.

Emily Secomb enjoys writing fiction, especially romance. She currently attends college and is studying to be a medical interpreter for the deaf.

Ingrid Shelton is a retired teacher/librarian and a freelance writer. Her hobbies are organic gardening and walking.

Patti Shene is Vice-President of Written World Communications and Executive Editor for *Starsongs* magazine. Her work has appeared in local publications and on www.Devokids .com.

Tamara L. Stagg is a freelance writer who lives with her husband and two children in Knoxville, Tennessee. Her published works have appeared in a variety of Christian magazines.

Patricia L. Stebelton, author of *The Sleeping Matchbook* and *Watched,* lives with her husband, Dick, in Chelsea, Michigan. She is published in *Whispering in God's Ear* and Guidepost's *Extraordinary Answers to Prayer.*

Jessica Talbot and her husband live on a hobby farm in British Columbia. She has a passion for intercessory prayer and coordinates an email prayer group from home.

Marianna Carpenter Wieck took her walk into eternity in spring of 2005. Her daughter, Linda Rooks, helped her write her story.

Pam Zollman is the award-winning author of forty children's books. A former magazine editor, she speaks at writers' conferences, teaches writing classes, and works at LifeWay Christian Bookstore.

James Stuart Bell is a Christian publishing veteran and the owner of Whitestone Communications, a literary development agency. He is the editor of many story collections including the CUP OF COMFORT, LIFE SAVORS, and EXTRAORDINARY ANSWERS TO PRAYER series and the coauthor of numerous books in THE COMPLETE IDIOT'S GUIDE series. He and his family live in West Chicago, Illinois.